Also by Mandy Aftel:

When Talk Is Not Cheap
(with Robin Lakoff)

Death of a Rolling Stone:
The Brian Jones Story

The Story of Your Life

Becoming the Author
of Your Experience

Mandy Aftel

Simon & Schuster
New York London Toronto Sydney Tokyo Singapore

SIMON & SCHUSTER
Rockefeller Center
1230 Avenue of the Americas
New York, NY 10020

SIMON & SCHUSTER and colophon are registered trademarks of
Simon & Schuster Inc.

Designed by Levavi & Levavi

Manufactured in the United States of America

1   2   3   4   5   6   7   8   9   10

Library of Congress Cataloging-in-Publication Data
Aftel, Mandy.
The story of your life : becoming the author of your experience /
Mandy Aftel.
p.   cm.
Includes bibliographical references.
1. Personal construct therapy. 2. Self-help techniques. 3. Self-perception.
4. Self-actualization (Psychology). I. Title.
RC489.P46A38   1996
616.89'14—dc20   95-25477
CIP

ISBN 0-684-81557-5

Acknowledgments

It is difficult to adequately thank Robin Lakoff, Todd Gitlin, Ron Hansen, and Laura Strausfeld who read this manuscript (many times) and made many valuable suggestions. Each offered generous support to my ideas and to me every step of the way. I am deeply grateful to my agent, Peter Matson, who believed in me from the start and never flinched. I would also like to thank Art Spiegelman for his early support for this book and the Salman Rushdie quote. Victoria Gill helped get my ideas out of my head and onto the page; and thanks go to Naomi Lucks for all her editorial skill, especially with titles. I want to express my pleasure in working with my editor, Becky Saletan, and my gratitude for her care and concern for my ideas, for her careful and respectful editing, and for championing this work. To Denise Roy, my appreciation for all her phone calls, hard work, and generosity. I thank Sister Eileen and Sister Kathleen O'Hanlon for their great kindness toward me. And, lastly, my daughter, Chloe, for the continual joy she brings into my life.

For Nancy La Rose

Contents

Those who do not have power over the story that dominates their lives, power to retell it, rethink it, deconstruct it, joke about it, and change it as times change, truly are powerless, because they cannot think new thoughts.

—Salman Rushdie,
"One Thousand Days
in a Balloon,"
New York Times,
December 12, 1991

Introduction

The quest for a story is the quest for a life.
—Jill Johnston,
"Fictions of the Self,"
*New York Times Book
Review,* April 25, 1993

Is This My Beautiful Life?

You may find yourself behind the wheel of a large automobile
You may find yourself in a beautiful house with a beautiful
   wife
You may ask yourself, well, how did I get here? . . .
You may tell yourself, this is not my beautiful house
You may tell yourself, this is not my beautiful wife . . .
—Talking Heads,
"Once in a Lifetime"

We want life to be simple. We want our answers
to be easy, our princes to be charming, our endings to be
happy. But like it or not, as long as we are alive, life will continue to throw things at us—good, bad, and indifferent, at
every moment and from every angle. As Roseanne Rosean-
nadanna used to say, "It's always something!"

We should know this by now, but most of us don't.
Whether you are twenty, forty, sixty, or eighty, you have undoubtedly had the experience of surveying your life, as if for

the first time, and asking, How did I get here? Why did this happen to me?

Why We Tell Stories

I have been a psychotherapist for almost twenty years. And almost every day of every week, I have listened to people tell me about their lives. Again and again, I am struck by how like short stories these tales are. I hear stories of love, loss, intrigue, and existential angst. My clients tell me of romance, adventure, mystery, despair. They portray themselves as heroes, victims, spurned lovers, cads. They describe the other characters who play large and small roles in their lives—the wonderful new boyfriend, the nagging wife, the smothering parent, the grateful friend, the attractive coworker, the unfeeling bureaucrat.

When I began to be aware that my clients were telling me stories with plot and narrative and character, I also became aware that I was doing the same thing—almost every minute of every day of my life. Regardless of our writing talent, in our daily lives we are all ad hoc novelists. We tell the stories of our lives in job interviews and blind dates, at slumber parties and in therapy. We tell our stories to our friends, to our neighbors, to our parents, to ourselves, and to strangers on the bus. We are both the heroes of our own plots and their creators. In a very real sense, we are the authors of our own lives.

Every person's story contains the elements of good literature: major themes, plot complications, subplots, protagonists, antagonists, major and minor characters. The narrators, whether they know it or not, shape their stories toward certain, often predetermined ends—toward love, toward mastery, or toward loss. In the process, they grapple with life's inevitable complications (money, escape, sex, children) and the traumas (death, illness, accident, acts of God)—that can pick up our well-crafted plots and smash them to bits.

Somewhere along the way, I consciously began to treat these stories as literature: I listened for the places where the narrative didn't make sense because the author had left out a key plot point, or had ascribed actions to a character that just didn't fit, or had distorted a circumstance to force the story into shape. I was the editor who could read my clients' stories objectively, pointing out patterns and themes, helping them to see how they might redefine one-dimensional characters and redirect stale plots to create a more complex, more satisfying narrative. As we worked in this way, my clients began to see that they were indeed narrating their stories, and that they could reframe the events of their lives, opening up plot possibilities they had never dreamed possible.

This can happen for a deceptively simple reason: *The way we describe our lives and understand them is ultimately and inextricably connected to the way we live them.* As we begin to become aware of the narrative patterns around which we structure our lives, we learn how to take charge, revise, refine, and even completely rewrite them. The one-dimensional stories that we often cling to—simplistic tales of blame, guilt, hopelessness, anger—can be transformed through time, work, and attention into subtle and richly textured narratives.

If you pay close attention to the stories others tell you, you will learn volumes about what they think and what they believe. And as you begin to pay attention to your own stories and what they say about you, you will enter into the exciting process of becoming, as you should be, the author of your own life, the creator of your own possibilities.

You are the narrator of your own stories, and as you change, your plot will also change. As you begin to see the possibility of new and different stories in your future, as you feel able to make the first step toward confronting a problem, you will change your plot. As you learn how to reframe the events of your life into a story different from the one you've been telling, you will change your plot. As you begin to see the roles that other people play in your life, and the roles you play in their lives, your life will be filled with the richness and complexity of good literature rather than the stale clichés and hackneyed plots of soap opera.

Wherever you are in your life right now, *you can change your plot*. I know this is true because I see it happen every day. As author Gail Sheehy said, "Millions of people entering their forties and fifties today are able to make dramatic changes in their lives and habits, to look forward to living decades more in smoothly functioning bodies, with agile minds—so long as they remain open to new vistas of learning and imagination and anticipate experiences yet to be conquered and savored."

The ideas in this book are what I believe: they are how I live my life and what I give to my clients as a therapist. This book will not offer you ten simple steps to fulfillment, or ten easy answers to life's problems, or a Prozac-like prescription to smooth life's road. It will offer you a way to appreciate the full spectrum of life—a way to see that you and the people you love and hate are complex characters rather than one-dimensional heroes and villains, a way to craft subtle nuances of possibility and change rather than awaiting inevitable tragedy or the happy ending that can never really be. Finally, it offers you a way stop letting others write the story of your life, and to forever more tell your own tales.

How to Use This Book

I have specialized in therapy for artists and writers and have worked with many writers to deal with problems in both their personal life and their work. What continually strikes me is the interconnection between the two: that all the work is ultimately autobiographical if you know how to read the author. Certain issues, themes, and plots recur and are reworked again and again, just as they are in therapy. I do not want to suggest that good writing is merely therapy. But writing remains one of the great pathways to the psyche.

I agree with novelist and writing instructor Anne Lamott,

when she observes, "The purpose of most great writing seems to be to reveal in an ethical light who we are." The plots I am talking about in this book are character driven. A character-driven plot unfolds as you understand your own character and the character of other people in your life. You make your life happen, your life doesn't make you happen. If you feel you play a part in creating your life, you can play a part in changing it.

When you make a commitment to understanding yourself and others, and to being able to read the answers to such questions as "Why did he do that?" "Why did I say that?" "What does that mean about me?" you will gain in understanding and experience, and your plot will continue to change and to grow. Character growth means that you have learned from experience. Life is not static but, rather, always evolving—your relationships change, your beliefs change, your views of yourself change, what you think you want changes. With these changes comes a revised understanding of who we are and how our interpersonal world is constructed. As you begin to see the events of your past arranged in a meaningful story, you begin to understand why you react as you do.

At the end of most of the chapters in this book, you will find exercises that will help you to think narratively about your experiences and to apply the principles of plotting to your own life. You certainly do not have to do these exercises to benefit from the ideas in this book. But actually writing about your plots and the characters in your life can help you understand these concepts in a deeper way, and can suggest changes in your plot that you may not otherwise have contemplated. So my suggestion to you is not just to read the exercises and think about the answers, but actually to *write them down*. Keep a special notebook for this purpose. Commit your ideas to paper, read them, and think about them.

Learning to recognize the elements of plot in your daily thinking can open up options you never thought possible. Actually plotting your life—not manipulating and scheming, but consciously structuring and mapping it out—multiplies your possibilities, naturally and joyously. When you find yourself stuck doing the same old things, instead of despairing you will be able to see how to rewrite the possibilities. When you find yourself repeating unsatisfactory patterns again and again with your best friend, your lover, your mother, you will recognize how you have underwritten a major character and begin to look for depth and nuance you had never noticed before. In short, when you begin to learn to listen to your own story, you will be amazed at how interesting your life is!

Some authors figure out all the twists and turns their plots will take before they begin to write. But great writers often report that despite what they had planned at the beginning, the characters soon begin to take on a life of their own. Even as they are writing the story, they are looking forward as eagerly as any reader to find out what will happen.

Our lives should be just this way. If we are living out someone else's story, or an old, hackneyed, plot of our own that allows for few deviations, surprises, or new characters, no one will want to hear our stories—least of all ourselves. But when we are actively involved in writing our own stories—determining plot, bringing in new characters, allowing familiar characters to change and grow—then our stories come alive, and so do we.

When you think of your life as a plot, you can pull back as a camera does at the end of a film and grasp the larger perspective, see the larger drama you are enacting. You can notice the repeatable themes and elements in the stories you tell about your life, and in this way you can begin to redirect the action.

In this book you will find the tools you need to transform that overworked melodrama you have been writing for the last thousand years into a tale of wonder and mystery told in language that is all your own. It will be a story of your own life that you can't put down, a story full of surprises that always leaves you saying, "I wonder what will happen next."

1

Every Day I Write the Book:
The Stories of Our Lives

> There is a kind of arranging and telling and choosing of detail—of narration, in short—which we must do so that one day will prepare for the next day, one week prepare for the next week. . . . To the extent that we impose some narrative form onto our lives, each of us is in the ordinary process of living a fitful novelist.
> —Phyllis Rose, *Parallel Lives*

Joe was a computer programmer in his late thirties who had come to me because of problems in his marriage. One day, he sat down hard in the chair in my office and declared, "My wife is so cold, I can't stand it." I was intrigued: I asked him if he could tell me a story that would make me see her coldness. This is what he told me:

Last night when I came home from work, it was late—I got stuck in traffic—and I was feeling miserable because I had just heard that Gary, my college roommate, had died of a massive heart attack during a bike trip. God, it was unbelievable. He was only thirty-six, like me, and he was in much better shape than I am. I was feeling terrible about it, and I told my wife the news the minute I hit the door. But instead of sympathizing with me, Barbara just said, "Oh well, don't feel bad, it's not like you see him every day. You haven't seen him in years." Then she launched into all the problems she had with the contractor that day—we're remodeling. That made me see what a cold bitch she is. She doesn't care about anyone but herself. I really think I need to leave her and get on with my life.

In his story, Joe was a warm, caring, sympathetic character and his wife was uncaring and self-centered. The plot was clearly headed toward loss—loss of love, loss of relationship, loss of emotional support—and Joe couldn't see any other possibilities. Not surprisingly, he felt angry, sad, and lonely. When I asked him if he had communicated these feelings to his wife, he said no, he didn't think she would be interested. Without much enthusiasm, he finally agreed to tell her how he felt, and be open to her response. This was the story he told me at our next session:

Well, I did what you asked. I told Barbara that the way she had pushed away Gary's death made me feel angry and isolated. She burst into tears. I was really surprised. She said she couldn't stand to see me so upset, that it made her think maybe I was worried that I would die suddenly, and she was trying to distract me from my feelings. And she didn't want to think that this could happen to me, either—it seemed easier for her to push the thought away. Then she suddenly gave me a big hug, and apologized. We both cried for a while. . . . I don't know. I'm beginning to think that maybe if we just opened up to each other, our relationship might get back on track.

Now Joe's story was no longer about loss but about hope—about rekindled romance and a second chance for happiness. His own character had become less victimized and more vulnerable, and his wife had been transformed from a cold bitch to a confused, caring, protective, loving friend. He had revised the direction of his plot from a story ending in divorce to the possibility of change and continuity.

This sort of storytelling doesn't happen only in therapy. We tell stories about our lives every day, often many times a day. We can't help it—bald statements about someone's character, like Joe's assertion about his wife, mean almost nothing unless they are supported by a story.

For example, your lover tells you, "My boss is a monster." Why?

"Because he criticized me in front of the whole committee for losing the project plans, and when Anne told him that she remembered giving the plans to him herself, he never even apologized to me."

Or you tell your coworker, "My friend Sally is a saint." Why?

"Because she made a dinner party for me the other night. She was worried about how withdrawn I had become since my mother died a couple of months ago. She wanted to bring me back to the world." These stories describe not only the events that transpired but also a piece of how their narrators see the world—that a rude boss is a nightmare, that a supportive friend is one who tries to draw you out socially.

We tell the stories of who we are in bits and pieces to friends and lovers and even strangers, but we also tell them to ourselves and enact the plots we devise. The story we tell others may be wildly different from the one we tell ourselves, but there is always a narrative thread connecting the major themes: childhood, education, romantic attachments, career, religious beliefs, recreational interests—the list is as varied as our lives. These powerful narratives serve not only to inform, entertain, and seduce others but also to create, maintain, reveal, and defend ourselves. Do we see ourselves as a victim, a hero, a lovable loser, a misunderstood genius? How do we interpret the circumstances we created and those that befell us?

You may not think of the stories you tell about yourself as stories you made up, but in a sense they are. Without a narrative thread—a plot—the events in your personal history are unrelated, like items like a shopping list. To make an intelligible account of our experiences is a human need, almost as basic as breathing. Sometimes we cast ourselves in too large or too small a role in the events of our lives. For example, you may have seen yourself as responsible for the breakup of your parents' marriage (as playing a large role), when in fact the problem was between the two of them and began long before you were even born (when you really had a very small role). Or because you are unable to imagine yourself in a larger role, you may decide to keep your job as a reporter on a small hometown newspaper instead of risking a change in your self-concept and going for a job as a *New York Times* correspondent.

Plots and Subplots

Your *plot* is the story you impose, retrospectively, on the events of your life. Plot includes not only a chronological sequence of events but causes and effects as well. Plot is the governing principle of development and coherence in your story, the pattern you use to select what best portrays your life to yourself and others. Without a plot, the things that happen to us are just a jumble of unconnected events. For example:

I got up late.
I went to work.
At lunch, a car almost hit me.

My boss yelled at me.
I got a lot accomplished.

For these events to make sense, you need to tie them together with a story:

I had the most unbelievably weird day. First, I forgot to set my alarm clock last night so I had only fifteen minutes to get up and get ready for work. I was frantic! I didn't even have time for a cup of coffee. When I got to work, I couldn't get much done because I was so out of it. So I took an early lunch, figuring I could at least catch up on coffee, and I was so preoccupied I walked right in front of a car. Well, that got the adrenaline running. Now I was wide awake. When I got back to work my boss yelled at me for taking an early lunch—he had every right to be mad, but I didn't appreciate being yelled at. Frankly, though, I was so glad to be alive anywhere—even at work—that I just tried to shine it on. I got right to work and finished up every project on my desk. Not too bad.

Another person, or yourself on another day, might take the same events and make a different plot out of them:

I am so stupid. I forgot to set my alarm clock again, and I overslept by an hour. By the time I got to work I couldn't even think. My office mate told me I needed food to get the blood sugar to my brain. So I took an early lunch, and as usual I wasn't watching where I was going, and dumb old me, I crossed the street on a red light and was almost killed. It probably would have been better if the car had hit me, because when I got back to work my boss was furious at me for leaving. I know he thinks I never do anything right, and this just proved his point. So I worked extra hard the rest of the day and finished all the projects on my desk, but I know he's still keeping his eye on me.

What Is a Story?

Stories are the interlocking narratives we use to hold our plots together. For example, if your basic plot is, "I'm so stupid, I never do anything right," you would tell the second story in the example above. Earlier, Joe told the story of his wife's reaction to Bob's death to illustrate the plot, "My wife's a cold person."

E. M. Forster describes the difference between plot and story succinctly: "The king died and then the queen died" is a story. "The king died and then the queen died of grief" is a plot. The sequence of the story is preserved in the plot, but a sense of causality overshadows it. Or again: "The queen died, but no one knew why, until it was discovered that it was of grief at the death of the king." This is a plot with mystery in it, a form capable of high development. Consider the death of the queen. If it is in a story we say, "And then?" If it is in a plot we ask, "Why?"

In literature, plays, and movies, the plot is the underlying structure that holds the action together and gives it direction. It can be as simple as a romance—boy meets girl, boy loses girl, boy gets girl—or as convoluted as a murder mystery. In fiction, the author is free to manipulate events and characters to suit the needs of the plot.

Unfortunately, life does not afford us this luxury. There is a very big difference between plot in literature and plot as we live our lives. Plot in fiction is constructed by the author and laid out for the reader. Plot in life is more like a mystery we try to solve by telling and retelling stories. Although you can make stories about what happens to you, *your life is not fiction*—it's quite real. In fiction, stories have a beginning, a middle, and an end. In life, our stories are always open-ended, evolving and changing to reflect our own growth.

Here are some key points to remember about the nature of plotting:

- All plots are character driven. We use plotting to understand character—our own, and everyone else's.
- Plot is a process, not a result. It is never complete as long as you are gathering experience, reflecting on it, letting it shape the way you see yourself, and testing that portrayal of yourself against your inner listener and others' experience of you.
- Plots are thoughts, feelings, actions, and events that we shape into narratives through language. Consciously or unconsciously, we organize our experiences into stories that present a certain view of ourselves. These are the versions we believe in and tell others when we share our experiences. Words help us to develop and to crystallize our sense of who we are. We create, define, and revise our identities by choosing what to include in our plots and how to express it.
- Successful plotting depends on our willingness to scrutinize our stories, look for patterns that reveal the deeper story we are enacting, and rethink the reasons we behave as we do—reasons we have taken at face value. Unsuccessful plotting, by contrast, takes no thought at all.
- All of our plots are formed in retrospect—we look back on the events of our lives and impose a meaning on them. To form plots, we include certain events from our lives and ignore others. You probably do not have a complete autobiographical narrative ready to relate to anyone who asks, but you certainly have recounted chapters of it: "How I Learned You Can Only Depend on Yourself"; "How I Decided I Wanted to Have Children"; "How I Decided to Get Married"; and so on.
- When you first meet someone you are interested in getting to know, you exchange stories about yourselves. When you talk to your friends or family, you give them accounts of your experiences that present you in a certain light. When you reflect privately on your life, you see it as a story in which you (and others) play certain roles.

Whether you like it or not, your plot is your own. You fit new experiences into it, and you understand your past in terms of its structure. It is your way of making your life coherent and interpretable. And it determines the types of experiences you can seek, tolerate, and survive.

The Hackneyed Plot: Life as a Cliché

Life, of course, is not just *your* story. We interact with many people every day, friends and strangers, and the directions of our plots intersect constantly, creating new problems and possibilities. People whom we love often compel us to play a role in *their* plots, and sometimes the roles that others have written for us eclipse the plot we have been dreaming for ourselves. Margie, for example, tells this story:

> When I was in high school, I loved to draw. And I always thought that when I graduated I would move to the city, live in a loft, and be a painter. I could really see myself living there— I'd get a job as a waitress, I'd shop for clothes in thrift stores, and I'd eat a lot of rice and vegetables to save money. My mother liked the idea of art, but she had always planned that I'd go away to college—to her college—and live in the same sorority that she joined when she was in school. And she wanted this for me so much—she really loves me, and she was scared of what might happen to me in the city, by myself— and I thought, maybe she's right. So I never did get to live in that loft. And I always wondered how my life might have been different if I had.

Margie's story is actually fairly common. Taking charge of our own lives can mean hard work. When we get tired, or when we don't have enough self-esteem to carry us through, we tend to let go of the reins, allowing ourselves to be pulled in directions we never intended to go. The truth is that if you aren't actively creating your own plot—even if it's one you don't much like—one will be constructed for you: by your family, by the movies, by advertising, by your own inertia. Inevitably, these ready-made plots will be hackneyed—get married, have kids, move to the suburbs; go to law school, get a job in a large firm, make a lot of money—because they lack the uniqueness that your own passions and preferences could have given them.

Plots are not scripts. A plot is a continuously evolving narrative arising out of self-knowledge and a sense of possibility. A script is a plan that we follow unthinkingly. Or, as Eric Berne, the founder of transactional analysis, has said, "A script is a life plan based on a decision made in childhood, reinforced by the parents, justified by subsequent events, and culminating in a chosen alternative."

For example, Wally followed his parents' script by marrying his high school sweetheart, becoming a pharmacist, working in his father's pharmacy, and taking over the business when his dad retired. He never gave a thought to what he might want to do with his life, or where his own interests might lie. As a consequence, he describes himself as "happy enough, I guess," but in reality he has always been plagued by vague feelings of longing and dissatisfaction that he has never been able to put a name to.

Between the script and the plot is the trite or hackneyed plot, which can arise from living out someone else's script. Because Wally has counted on someone else to determine his plot, he is doomed to a sit-com life. No matter how his life looks to people outside it, to him it will always look two-dimensional because he has not allowed himself to leave this predetermined track and really explore his own wants and needs.

Although we all try to some extent to fit into a role—the parent, the provider, the capable administrator—the person living out a trite plot cannot differentiate between himself and the role. To rewrite a trite plot, we need to allow some interplay between the role we have assumed and what's right for us. Wally, for example, may be thoroughly locked into being a pharmacist at this point, but some exploration may reveal to him a secret love for raising plants. If he took this seriously, he might begin to raise plants at home, and perhaps to take botany classes at night school. He might then feel his vague dissatisfaction with life turning into a new excitement about life's possibilities.

Many clichéd plots concern sex. They follow a predictable course, and the roles are constricting. Lorrie Moore, in her short story "How to Be an Other Woman," describes the irony of being trapped in a cliché:

> Shave your legs in the bathroom sink. Philosophize: You are a mistress, part of a great hysterical, you mean historical, tradition. Wives are like cockroaches. . . . They will survive you after a nuclear attack—they are tough and hardy and travel in packs. But right now they're not having any fun. . . . Some nights he says he'll try to make it over, but there's no guarantee. Those nights, just in case, spend two hours showering, dressing, applying makeup unrecognizably, like someone in drag, and then, as it is late, and you have to work the next day, climb onto your bed like that wearing perfume and an embarrassing, long, flowing lacy bathrobe.

On the other hand, you can't, as the saying goes, tell a book by its cover. For example, you might assume that your friend Rebecca, who married for money, doesn't work, and spends her time going to "appointments," lives a terribly boring life, when in fact she's never been happier in her life: she's doing what she always wanted to do. What determines whether or not you are stuck in a clichéd plot isn't the plot itself but the degree to which it expresses your authentic self. If you feel that you're doing everything "right" but nothing seems to be working out, if you feel constantly dissatisfied with your relationships or unable to express yourself, it may be time to revise your plot.

Like it or not, we all get our share of loss to deal with. It's easy to check out and just go along with the program, but sooner or later the lid will blow off a hackneyed plot: a child will commit suicide, a husband will abandon the family to search for gold in Alaska, a respected lawyer will be sidelined by alcohol abuse, a dutiful daughter will be arrested for pandering.

From my work, it is clear to me that people experience much more remorse for the results of their passivity and inertia than for the failed risks they have undertaken. Although the price for action, when it goes wrong, is obvious, the price of inaction is much higher. Before you know it, your life has gone by. No matter what you believe about life after death or the possibility of reincarnation, one fact is indisputable: you get only one opportunity to live *this* life. Experience offers us, the narrators and principal characters of our own never-ending stories, countless opportunities to learn and grow. There is no role from which we cannot learn. In this respect we are always works in progress.

Exercises for Chapter 1

Your Cast of Characters

Write out a cast of characters from your life, limiting it to ten people. Include those who have most strongly affected your life, either positively or negatively—parents, siblings, children, teachers, heroes, lovers, mates, maids, grandparents, friends, bosses. Write a capsule description of each, emphasizing his or her importance to your plot. For example:

John, my ex-husband, who convinced me for five years that I was at fault for everything that was wrong in our marriage.

Grandma Pat, my mother's mother, who was always kind to me, even when I accidentally broke her favorite vase.

Keep this exercise at the front of your notebook—you will be using it throughout this book.

This Is Your Life: Casting Yourself

You are, of course, the main character in your own life. But because we live inside ourselves, it can be difficult to get a handle on who we are. Get some perspective on what you think of your own character by answering the following questions:

1. Who would play you in a movie about you?
2. If you wrote your own autobiography, what would the title be?
3. Who would you most like to be (living or dead, real or imaginary)?
4. Who do you think is the opposite of you?
5. Imagine that you believe in the idea that souls are reincarnated in four stages: from the plant world, to the animal world, to the human world, to an unknown world. Now describe yourself in each world—as a plant (fruit, vegetable, tree, and so on), as an animal, in your present human form, and in the form you see yourself becoming.

Your Important Life Events

Make a list of the important turning points in your life. List the obvious ones (your parents' divorce, going away to school, your first job) and the not so obvious ones, including those with no observable signs (for example, the day you realized you no longer believed in God).

1. Choose one of these major turning points and briefly describe how it altered your character.
2. Describe the changes in your life that looked like changes but were more deeply just a way of staying the same.
3. List the events in your life that occurred only once.
4. List the events that seem to repeat over and over again in your life.
5. Make a list of the things in life that you wanted and have gotten. List how any of them have made you happy.
6. What is the one thing that would never happen to you in a million years? Imagine that this actually did happen to you. How did you react?
7. How would you describe where you are at present in your life? What about your life do you like best? If you could have had any kind of life you wanted, what would it look like?

What's Your Story?

We all tell stock stories about ourselves. Briefly record (one paragraph) the story you tell the following people about yourself at your first meeting:

A potential mate
Someone you'd like to work for
Someone you'd like to have work for you
A psychotherapist

2

The Telltale Self:
The Narrator

The self is a telling.
—Roy Schafer

You are the narrator of your own story. In fact, whether you are aware of it or not, you probably can't help telling your story. We tell stories to anyone who will listen: about our self to our listening self, to intimate friends, and to the outside world. Even if we think we're telling the same story to everyone, it will differ according to who's listening.

We tell stories to our listening self about different aspects of ourselves. This is often called *internal dialogue*. To have self-knowledge, we have to make that story as truthful as possible. For example, if I am honest with myself, I have to admit that since Ralph dumped me, I was imagining him in bed every morning with a Cindy Crawford lookalike. What a relief it was when I heard that he went back to his overweight and nagging wife! When I tell the same story to others, it is in a much more edited and sanitized version—I say that I'm glad that since I dumped Ralph, he was able to go back to his wife. In the private version of my story, I can be as vindictive as I feel. In the public version, however, I present myself in a more socially acceptable light.

When we tell these edited versions of our stories we cover up our wounds or areas of instability, either lightly or with a full suit of armor. Our purpose is to both reveal and conceal ourselves. This is the same idea as sexy lingerie—and the analogy is apt, for the function of the stories we tell others is to seduce.

Core Beliefs: Just Who Do You Think You Are?

These two kinds of storytelling—private and public—may differ to a degree, but the themes, issues, and cruxes that embody our core beliefs about our selves in the world and how we think the world works permeate all our stories, no matter whom the audience is. These core beliefs usually come from our experience in our family—what they said or did and the ways we were made to feel about what they said or did. They may also come from teachers or peers, or from watershed experiences like the death of a parent or a divorce. Those experiences were perceived as lessons, and what we learned from them is often painful. Such experiences lay the groundwork for a repeated and subtly (or not so subtly) reinforced way of being regarded by significant others.

These beliefs become a given in our psychological repertoire because they remain unexamined. Examples of core beliefs include the following:

I am wrong to put my own needs before those of another person.
No matter how good things are, a disaster is always waiting.
I can't trust anyone.

My flaws are totally unacceptable to others.
I must be perfect or I am worthless.
I must please others to avoid attack.
I'm okay if I'm better than others.
I must control myself at all times.
Whatever happens, I learn from it.
I can handle what comes up.

As this list illustrates, our core beliefs tend to be negative.

Sometimes the ongoing emotional atmosphere of your family, peers, or schoolroom is so salient that it becomes the organizing principle for your view of yourself. You take it in and believe it describes you. The self—that is, the "I" that narrates your story—doesn't question this principle, and doesn't realize that it is editing your experience to fit. Once the core belief is in place, all thoughts and reality radiate from that point.

In the title story of her collection, *Cowboys Are My Weakness,* Pam Houston comments on how one can structure an entire reality around a misconception:

> I thought about the way we invent ourselves through our stories, and in a similar way, how the stories we tell put walls around our lives. And I think that may be true about cowboys. That there really isn't much truth in my saying cowboys are my weakness; maybe, after all this time, it's just something I've learned how to say.

An example: Sarah was an outstanding athlete, but she was an anomaly in a family of academics who prized intellectual achievements. Even though she excelled at field hockey and basketball, her family made her feel unworthy and substandard.

> My dad was a well-known anthropologist, my mom was one of the youngest physicists, male or female, to get her own lab, and my sister got straight A's all the way through school. I was

interested only in sports—my grades were okay, but nothing special. My sister got all the strokes for being smart, and I just got their puzzled looks. I guess they couldn't relate to me on any level—how could they have raised this girl jock? My dad didn't even watch football on TV. I grew up feeling like a stupid freak.

Sarah grew up with the core belief "I'm stupid and unworthy." Later in life, she unconsciously created and supported ways to make that belief true about her. She skipped classes in college and was forced to drop out, and she took what her family considered to be menial jobs to support herself. She never returned to school, and eventually took a job in the gift shop of a ski resort.

The lens through which the narrator looks can be so tightly focused that no new information can enter. This technique for turning a silk purse into a sow's ear works as follows: You perceive how people act and react to you through the lens of your past, the core belief you developed in your family. All roads lead back to confirming that view of yourself. Once the theme or motif is in place, such as Sarah's "I am stupid," you interpret your life as having a "stupid" plot. This causes you to see your past behavior only as stupid, rather than all the other things it might be. Further, it causes you to make choices designed to avoid exposing your "stupidity." The theme is self-fulfilling—your isolation limits you and, in effect, makes you stupid.

If someone speaks to you intelligently about something you read, or indicates that your response to a situation was appropriate, you think that they are just being polite, or they feel sorry for you, or they must say that to everyone, or they have bad taste, and so forth. Another technique by which you may confirm this image of yourself is to seek approval from hypercritical people: for example, to pursue potential partners who find you too tall, too fat, too bookish, too emotional, too mousy. In ways like these, you shrink the world and accept only evidence that supports your flawed view of yourself, allowing no new information to be processed.

Flawed assumptions often get in the way of living an authentic life. In order to locate what you really want, you must first examine what you have received. Then, as with spring cleaning, you must prepare to give away those things that no longer fit. Consider Rachel's story:

> My mother always told me that life without children is empty and that was why she had six kids. I got married in my late thirties and always thought I, too, would have a family. But Lester was still in graduate school and it wasn't a good time to start a family. Then last year I found out that he was having an affair and really there was little to save from our marriage; we were poorly suited to one another. The hardest thing, though, was for me to give up the promise of a family. Now I am forty-three and have to face the fact that I may never have children. I travel a lot for my job, and maybe I have not found a situation conducive to childbearing because I really don't want to have one of my own.

When we test flawed assumptions we change the narrator's story and the narrator's place in that story. For example, a person who thinks he or she is ugly can have only certain kinds of stories. No matter how many people tell you that it's all in your head, you will never believe them. You cannot be rescued by others from this type of story making. No one will come along and make you beautiful, or athletic, or educated. You have to rescue yourself.

For example, in high school, Ethan had a terrible case of acne. He felt that girls were grossed out by his complexion, and he developed the idea that he was homely and unattractive. At the age of thirty, however, a successful career as a research scientist had given him the self-confidence (and faith in the experimental method) that he needed to try to change his self-image. As an "experiment," Ethan decided to try to make himself more attractive. He started working out at a gym, got a personal shopper at the department store to help him select more flattering clothes, and generally worked on the idea that a more attractive version of himself was waiting to emerge. As Ethan's self-esteem improved, he found that others were reacting to him differently, and this new evidence in turn began to correct his negative self-regard.

Stories about the self radiate from a feeling of self-esteem. Your possible story, your position in it, and the stories that can be attracted to yours all come from your level of genuine positive self-regard. Let's say you constantly cast yourself in stories where you play the role of the victim. When you realize your contribution to these stories, a shift occurs in the stories themselves, because a symbiotic relationship exists between the narrator and the story. They are not divisible; there is no story without a self to tell it and act it out. *As the self—the narrator—evolves, so does the plot.*

Point of View: How Do You See the World?

Tangential to our core belief is the point of view that we assume, as the narrator, the stance we take when we tell our stories. Most of us narrate our story either from the short-sighted point of view of a child or from the point of view of a rigid, moralistic adult; a lucky few are able to integrate the playfulness, vulnerability, and directness of a child with the understanding and tolerance of human differences that a wise adult possesses.

The Child's Point of View: Why Did You Do This to Me?

Many people, without realizing it, never get past the point of view of a child. Their stories are all about "me": "How could you do this to me?" That this should be so is not surprising; after all, the child's viewpoint is laid down first in the psyche, before the development of the vocabulary and the intellectual sophistication that would permit flexibility and distance.

The child's point of view admits no empathy for adults, no understanding of compromise, no reality principle, no sense that the child's needs are not the most pressing, no concept of "later." Other people appear powerful, without fear or weakness. When children draw pictures of their parents, they may depict small bodies with enormous heads, or figures taller than a tree or house nearby. This represents not just the physical but the psychological perspective of the child.

Of course, there are both negative and positive aspects to the child's viewpoint. The negative aspects include being self-centered, afraid, impatient, and uncompromising, while the healthy, positive aspects include a sense of playfulness, pleasure, vulnerability, and innocence.

Generally, however, when you inhabit the child's point of view, you see others as more powerful and less vulnerable than yourself. Children see themselves as *someone to whom things are done.* Adult narrators who see life from the child's point of view, then, see themselves as victims, with a resulting diminution of plot possibilities.

The Adult's Point of View: Life Is More Complex Than It Seems

We can never completely lose the child's perspective, nor would that be desirable. As we establish an adult viewpoint—marked by self-knowledge, practicality, patience, experience of human nature (from reading others), and compassion regarding others' weaknesses and fears—our task is to integrate the two. The narrator must balance the two viewpoints and provide a connection—the narrative—that permits the adult and child to talk to each other, since to lack either is a distortion.

Becoming an adult involves achieving a sense of mastery. Just as an infant experiences a thrill upon first sitting upright or standing, a healthy adult point of view involves a shift in perspective, and the liberation of realizing that other points of view are possible. Not all adults achieve this, however; instead they may be stuck in an unhealthy rigidity, judgmentalness, or coldness. Clearly, the combination of an unhealthy child's point of view with an unhealthy adult's point of view is a nightmare! But when a healthy adult point of view is informed by a healthy child's point of view, then open delight and playful engagement with life is a joy to behold.

What the Narrator Does

The narrator has many separate voices; some contradictory, some harmonious. The narrator can both want to be a doctor *and* want to take a banana boat to Brazil. In one sense, the narrator is a sort of receptionist at an internal switchboard to which these different aspects of the self call in with their demands and suggestions. The narrator is the operator who connects these parts of the self and gets them to have conversations with one another. Only the narrator oversees this crucial process of integration.

The narrator also balances competing demands. Only the narrator can say, "Part of me wants to never see that man again and the other part of me wants to move in with him." One role of the narrator is to contain all these disparate feelings and thoughts, and to provide a means for monitoring the conflicting parts of the self. This function of the narrator is like that of a politician who needs to know what his constituents want and tries to find a way to keep them all relatively satisfied. The narrator has a decision-making function—granting power, allocating resources, setting priorities, stalling impatient special interests. Further, the narrator-politician has to get reelected—that is, the narrator's version of things has to hold together and retain the primary storytelling function.

The narrator must continually ask the question, "What is reality?" and must be flexible enough to accept a kaleidoscope of answers. In Kurosawa's classic film *Rashomon,* for example, we see the same violent event depicted from the point of view of the perpetrator, the victim, witnesses, and so on, each of whom has a strikingly different slant on what happened. Kurosawa clearly makes the point that there is no absolute version of reality; it consists simply of the sum of competing individual experiences, which have certain irreducible elements in common. As narrator, our role is like that of the director of the film, whose vision contains all the realities, and who decides what to show and what to leave out.

If you have ever been in an intimate relationship, you have undoubtedly experienced this clash of realities. Clearly, it's necessary to pull back from the action sometimes to get a more detached overview. But while the capacity for self-observation can be very useful, if you don't dispense with it at times you will never have the experience of being wholly involved in anything. It is important sometimes just to *have* experiences and to filter them through the narrator's viewpoint later. In an essay titled "Storytelling," author Stephen Greenblatt tells this cautionary tale:

> One of the worst times I have ever been through in my life was a period—I cannot recall if it was a matter of days or weeks—when I could not rid my mind of the impulse to narrate my being. I was a student at Cambridge, trying to decide whether to return to America and go to law school or graduate school in English: "He's sitting at his desk, trying to decide what to do with his life," a voice—my voice, I suppose, but also not my voice—spoke within my head. "Now he's putting his head on his hand; now he is furrowing his brow; and now he is getting up to open the window". . . . I experienced the compulsive and detached narrativizing voice as

something that had seized me, that I could not throw off, for even my attempts to do so were immediately turned into narrative.

Clearly, too much self-observation is as bad as too little.

The Unreliable Narrator

There is a difference between the story as willfully presented by the narrator to listeners, and the story that is inadvertently exposed between the lines. The difference between the two is the domain of the unreliable narrator.

Your own story, like all autobiographies, is told in the first person: "I had a horrendous day today." This "I" who tells the story can never see events from an external viewpoint. On the other hand, the stories that you tell in the third person ("She had a big rip in the back of her dress and never even noticed it!"), although they capture the common denominator of experience and discount the special pleading of individuals, can be dispassionate, ironic, and distanced, thereby missing the emotional reality as it was experienced by the person to whom the story is most crucial.

All first-person narrators, by virtue of their outlook, are to some extent unreliable. When you read a novel, your job is to discover what the narrator wants to reveal and what he or she wants to protect and defend. One of the benefits of psychotherapy is that you have an opportunity to tell your true first-person narrative and can borrow an enlightened—if not omniscient—third-person perspective from your therapist. (Of course, a third-person perspective can be unreliable too, but for different reasons. Exercise care in whom you designate as your third-person narrator, whether it be a friend, therapist, or relative.)

The unreliable narrator is one who will not take responsi

bility, who won't examine his or her experiences and learn from them. This narrator takes a passive stance in the plot, and avoids seeing his or her own contribution to the present situation. For example:

> My roommate moved out on me today. Can you believe it? Now I'm stuck with double the rent. She said it was because I always leave hair in the sink, and that I never did my half of the cleaning up, but she's full of it. She's so meticulous no one could live up to her standards.

In contrast, reliable narrators have an active stance toward their lives and understand their part in shaping their life's plot. Such a narrator asks, "Okay, what did I bring to this situation? What did I choose and what was out of my control?" There is a shift here from "can't" to "won't," with *will* as the operative word. For example, "I can't leave this horrible job to do what I really want because I'm trapped and no one will support me" would change to, "I won't leave this job, although I find it unfulfilling, because I'm getting things from it—like medical insurance and a steady income—that I don't want to give up; but I'll make a plan to go back to school." As reliable narrators, we make the shift from a passive to an active role in what we choose and refuse.

Dramatic Style

The "what" of plot is partly determined by the cards fate deals you and the fixed circumstances of your life, but the "how" belongs in the domain of the narrator. The narrator's dramatic style—the tone or emotional atmosphere of your plot—can be very broadly defined as either *melodramatic* or *comic*. This is the predominant aspect of your narrative stance toward the events that fate, luck, chance, or circumstance sends your way. It is the pervasive emotional climate in which the events take place.

Dramatic style is about process and attitude, not about content and events. A very painful event, like your mate's leaving you for someone else, can seem ultimately humorous to one person and terminally tragic to another, depending on whether his or her dramatic style tends toward the melodramatic or the comic.

Melodramatic Style

People with a melodramatic style tend to be extreme and unsubtle. They concentrate on the bright and dark ends of the emotional spectrum without really seeing the shades of gray in between. Melodramatic narrators cannot laugh at themselves; their tone is heavy, burdened with tremendous emotional weight. Their focus is on themselves—no one else's pain appears as big, as real, or as important as their own. They have little or no sense of solidarity with others. They may be bitter, and their laughter is often at others' expense. This melodramatic style is akin to the child's point of view. For example:

> Darrin left last night and took all his dust-collectors. I hated all that stuff. What could have made me live with it for so long? I tried to improve his sense of taste, to introduce him to more intelligent people than those beer drinkers he hangs around with, but he's too dense to appreciate anything I have to offer. He just kept yelling at me to stop trying to change him. Can you believe that? He's impervious to change! I'm glad that jerk's out of my life.

Melodrama is marked by sentimentality, not true grief for the losses of the past. In the words of Marie-Louise von Franz, the Jungian psychoanalyst, "Where there is sentimen

tality, in general, there is also a certain amount of brutality.
[The Nazi general Hermann] Goering was a typical example,
for without a qualm he could sign the death sentence for three
hundred people, but if one of his birds died, then that old fat
man would cry. He is a classic example! Cold brutality is very
often covered up by sentimentality."

Comic Style

People with a comic narrative style, on the other hand, tend
to be hopeful and accepting about what happens in their
plots. They feel solidarity and kinship with others because
they see similarities rather than differences. Because they perceive the irony that reveals the difference between vanity and
accuracy, between life at face value and life in depth, and because they do not see their own concerns as paramount, their
laughter is not cruel and excluding but warm and inclusive of
others. They look for what was good about their experiences,
even if it wasn't what they expected it to be. They do not idealize what they *don't* have. They take responsibility for their
role in events and truly appreciate what they *do* have. For example:

> Darrin and I split up last week. He loaded his car up with all
> of his stupid toys and junk—I couldn't believe it, he looked
> like he was driving one of those clown cars. You couldn't even
> see him in there as he drove away. When I saw him go with all
> his stuff I realized that we never belonged together anyway;
> we're way too different. I like those clean lines, and he likes
> clutter. The house seemed really empty without all his stuff
> covering every surface, but I cuddled up with the two cats and
> a glass of wine and just figured, well, things couldn't get any
> worse!

Perhaps above all, the comic narrative style is marked by
hope. Hope is an open posture toward the future. According

to author Todd Gitlin, "The deepest hope has no definite object. Hopeful people are hopeful that things will turn out well, not that they will turn out well in a particular way."

The Importance of Language

Once we pluck an experience from the ebb and flow of our lives and express it meaningfully, that experience is irreversibly changed. Experience that we have talked about is deeply different from experience that we have never put into words.

Telling someone about your experience breathes new life into it, moving it out of the inchoate swirl of unconsciousness into reality. It takes on form, and allows us to examine it from all sides. For example, Georgia went to her twenty-year high school reunion, and returned home feeling vaguely sad. She didn't know why until she began to describe the reunion to her best friend:

There we were, all these dressed-up middle-aged people sitting at these separate tables in the banquet room of an airport hotel. I looked around me and all I could see were faces from high school, which had been about the lowest point of my life. And everyone was sitting at a table with their high school friends, staring at the people at the other tables but never really making contact—just like we did in high school! No wonder I feel so sad. That's exactly how I felt in the tenth grade.

Committing an experience to words not only fixes it within a verbal structure but also gives it a greater reality, because it determines how we will remember, regard, and communicate what transpired in the future.

Language gives meaning to experience. Changing the words we use to describe things can actually change what we want to do and what we think we are. This is true not only personally but culturally. We generally can't help but view ourselves through the lens of the current cultural metaphor. During the Enlightenment, for example, when science began to replace the Church as an authority, the human body was no longer described as a gift of God but as a clockwork mechanism—the heart was a pump, and the brain was full of cogwheels ticking our thoughts away. Today we use the new metaphor of cyberspace, and conceptualize the brain as a computer terminal with which we can jack into the universal network—which the psychologist Carl Jung described in the beginning of this century as the "collective unconscious." Clearly, what we think of as fixed reality is always open to reinterpretation.

By examining the way you tell your story and revising the way you narrate your life to yourself and others, *you can change the plot of your life.* As you learn new ways of looking at your situation, you evolve a new vocabulary to redescribe the events that make up your story. This new language permits you to portray yourself in ways that were not possible in your old plot, and eventually you enact the plot that your language permits you to devise: *when language changes, plot changes.*

For example, Terry, a thirty-year-old single mother, had gotten pregnant in high school. As a consequence, she dropped out before graduation and worked at a succession of menial jobs to support herself and her son. This is how she described her situation for many years:

> I couldn't get a break. I have such bad luck. I got pregnant the first time I had sex, and my boyfriend didn't want anything to do with me after that. My parents kicked me out. I had to quit school and get a job as a waitress in order to pay rent on the only crummy apartment I could find. My kid was screaming all the time. It was all I could do to get him to daycare, get to work, cook dinner, and crash. Nobody wants to go out with you when you have a kid, you know?

Now, at age thirty, she reframes her story in these words:

I thought I knew everything then, but I was really young. I got pregnant the first time I had sex—can you believe it never even occurred to me to use birth control? Thank God my boyfriend dumped me. If I'd have stayed with him I'd probably be dead by now. And life at home was pretty terrible. It didn't do much for my self-esteem. I hated my life at the time, but now, looking back, I can see that having to raise my son grew me up fast. I'm proud of what I did on my own, and I'm proud of the way he's turning out. I've been through the fire, and I know I'm a pretty strong person.

With this language, Terry's plot is no longer "I have terrible luck. I can't get a break," but, "I've been through the fire and I know I'm a pretty strong person." These words have enabled her to think about going back to finish school so that she can begin to get jobs that are more interesting to her, and they have enabled her son to be proud of what his mom has accomplished instead of being the reason for her rotten life.

Here's another example: Tom, fifty-five, was depressed because his golf game wasn't what it used to be. He could drive the ball only 150 yards instead of 200 yards, and he felt the decline of his game was an expression of his inevitable physical decline and ultimate mortality. Although he was a successful stockbroker, at the top of his form at work, he became obsessed with how poorly he performed on the links. His plot was, "I'm getting old and going downhill fast." He remembers:

My goddamn golf game! It was all I could talk about. Finally one of my oldest clients, who knows me pretty well, said, "Tom, you're looking at this thing all wrong. You should be savoring that 150 yards. Forget the 200 yards, that's over. Mourn it, say goodbye to it, and hold onto that 150, because 100 is coming next." That changed the whole picture for me. Yeah, I was getting worse—but I'd probably never be better! Sure, I'm gonna die, but I'm alive now and loving it. So what the hell?

The words we choose reveal our character and beliefs, how embedded we are in a given role. For example, a man who constantly says, "My wife did this, my wife did that," instead of using her name, reveals a certain pride of ownership, a wish to state "I'm married." Finding new words can give us a vantage point to look at causes and relations in a new way. Each change of vocabulary, such as from *Negro* to *black* to *African American,* embodies a difference in attitude. Saying *humankind* rather than *mankind* reminds us that women have an equal role with men in the life of the world. In the same way that we find our cultural attitudes changing with our terminology, we can actually change our lives by changing the words we use to tell our stories.

There are several ways to do this. First, we can redefine common words: Culturally speaking, the words *wife* and *mother,* for example, no longer define the same roles as they did at the turn of the century or even in the 1950s. Second, we can change the vocabulary we employ for charged experiences, employing more neutral and descriptive language in place of value-laden language: for example, changing "She's a slut" to "I feel jealous and hurt by the attention she gets from other men" changes not only the way others react to our stories but also the way we understand our lives.

Redescription offers us the opportunity to recast the plot elements to tell different stories. Often, glimpses in your plot of unrecognized or split-off parts of the self can prompt the need for redescription.

For example, Alberta bumped into a man who had been her best friend's lover. He made sexual advances toward her, and she rebuffed him. At their final meeting, he kissed her, and she was powerfully moved. They parted and she never saw him again. Alberta had never experienced a true romantic and passionate connection with a man, so she was unable to identify her feelings. She thought of him as a "womanizer" who was being disloyal to her friend. Only years later, when she had ceased to think of him as a womanizer and learned to see him as a sexual being, did she realize that this man had awakened her sexual passion. She was able to piece together in retrospect a new, infinitely more accurate interpretation of the events and characterization of herself as the narrator, with new plot options for herself in consequence. She realized that she was fearful of intensity, particularly of a sexual nature, and that she should examine her reactions over time in order not to respond merely from fear.

The terms by which we describe ourselves are always subject to change, but this does not mean that the earlier descriptions were wrong at the time. Later, you may reinterpret the meaning of certain events, thereby configuring a different pattern and plot.

However, not everything that happens is for the best, and redescription can be fraudulent as well as enlightening: "I didn't really want to go out with her anyway." "I can quit drinking whenever I want to." Understanding and accepting that some experiences *must* bring regret and remorse—and that these emotions are sometimes appropriate—is essential. You should aim for redescription that captures your loss, pain, and regret as well as your joys. With this in mind, there is a point where a description feels final in regard to some events. The kernel of your authentic truth has been discovered, and your narrative has a feeling of peace and completeness.

As you learn more about plotting, you will find that redescription occurs in bits and pieces, not in one fell swoop. You will not rewrite the story of your life overnight, as if you suddenly recovered from amnesia. Redescription, like plotting, is a process, not a result. Sometimes you feel that *now* you *truly* understand an event or a person, but that understanding may prove to be only partial. Understanding is ongoing and enlarging; no matter how much you know, there is always more to learn. You will return to some events again and again, each time seeing them in a more nuanced fashion. The self is never complete as long as it gains experience and understanding. Psychological development continues throughout adult life, and it should include some sense of affirming what is past, even if it was painful.

To take as much responsibility as possible for your own plot, and to read others' plots more accurately, is to take back the power you lost or gave away to a mistaken core belief that you formed as a child. To change your self-image is to change your narrative voice; to speak more as your authentic self is to become more your authentic self; and in so doing you will change your view of the world and your place in it. As philosophy professor Charles Taylor has said:

> Each of us has an original way of being human. . . . There is a certain way of being human that is *my* way. I am called upon to live my life in this way, and not in imitation of anyone else's. But this gives a new importance to being true to myself. If I am not, I miss the point of my own life, I miss what being human is for *me* . . . being true to my own originality, and that is something only I can articulate and discover. In articulating it, I am also defining myself. I am realizing a potentiality that is properly my own.

Exercises for Chapter 2

Finding Your Core Belief

Your core belief about yourself determines how you see yourself in the stories you tell. With an eye to determining your own core beliefs, reread what you wrote in the exercises in Chapter 1. Take a moment now to see if you can determine what at least one of your core beliefs may be. See if you can formulate a brief sentence that expresses your core belief about yourself. Try to choose one that feels the most deeply and generalizably true about you. (Turn back to pp. 35–36 for some common examples.)

Once you've written down your core belief, take a few minutes to consider it. Now write a brief story (one paragraph) from your life to support your core belief.

Changing Your Core Belief

Take the core belief you wrote down in the previous exercise and try changing the language in which you expressed it. For example, if you said, "Nobody knows who I really am," see how many ways you can reframe it with different words: "I never let anybody in." "I'm not as good as people think I am." "I'm much more creative than people think I am." "Nobody ever makes an effort to get to know the real me." Choose the statement that seems to resonate with you as the most truthful, and write a one-paragraph story to support it. Are you beginning to see possibilities for change?

Point of View

To be an authentic narrator, you will need to integrate multiple, often conflicting points of view. Try this:

1. Remember a painful incident from your childhood and write a brief paragraph recounting it from the child's point of view. (This should be easy—it's probably the way you have been telling this story for years.) Now tell the same story from your vantage point as an adult. Read both versions and note the differences in language and tone. Finally, try writing the story again to include both points of view. How has your story changed? How has your position in the story changed?

2. Remember a conflict you have recently had with a friend or coworker, for which you are convinced the other person is to blame. Write down what happened from your point of view. Now try your best to write the same story

from the other person's point of view. Can you see truth in both versions? Can you still make the other person wrong?

3. Take a moment to think about a story you always tell about a particular event in your life—the day you lost your virginity, the time your mother embarrassed you in front of your friends. Now think about how your best friend, your spouse, or your mother might tell that same story, and write it from that point of view. Because we are so close to our stories (they are, after all, us) it may be easier to do this in the third person. You might even break the story down into its component parts, without embellishment, and then see how you can put it back together. Redescribing your familiar story in this way will almost certainly put you in touch with aspects of your plot of which you were previously unaware.

4. Recall a situation where someone has hurt your feelings. Write the story from a child's point of view. Notice how you see the hurt as disproportionately large and yourself as extremely helpless. Now describe the hurtful event from the other person's point of view. Finally, describe the event from an adult point of view, looking at the character and intentions of all parties. How has the incident changed? Can you ever tell this story in the same way again?

Finding Your Style

Reread the stories you have written about yourself so far. How would you describe your style? Comic (hopeful, accepting, capable of laughing at yourself) or melodramatic (self-centered, unsubtle, emotionally extreme)? Write the same story in the opposite style from the one you used originally. Notice what you give more weight in each version, and what you leave out altogether. Notice how you feel about the events you are writing about. This is a particularly good exercise for a childhood experience. Do you see possibilities for change?

A Vocabulary Lesson

1. For one twenty-four-hour period, be mindful of your language. Notice when you label people ("my wife," "my child," "the girls at the office," "my husband is out with the boys"), and when you call them by name. Notice how many times you use words like *always, never, should, ought, stupid.* Write these instances in your notebook so that you have a record of them. What was your inner attitude when you used these phrases?
2. For another twenty-four-hour period, notice when other people use such labels. What are your feelings toward those people? What would you think of a character in a novel who talked this way?

3

Great Expectations:
What Motivates Our Plots

> A coherent life experience is not simply given, or a track
> laid down in the living. To the extent that a coherent
> identity is achievable at all, the thing must be made, a
> story-like production with many pitfalls, and it is con-
> stantly being revised, sometimes from beginning to end,
> from the vantage point of some new situation of the "I"
> that recollects.
>
> —Stephen Crites,
> *Storytime*

Although it seems that there must be an infinite
variety of plots for an infinite number of people, most plots
fall into one of three major categories: love, mastery, and loss.
Before we can understand how the plots work, though, we
need to look at the three major motives that drive them: self-
esteem, control, and separation.

Self-Esteem

Self-esteem—how deeply and genuinely you feel about yourself—is the most important of these motives. Self-esteem, the cornerstone of all your relationships, is created out of our core beliefs about the self. All love relationships mirror one's quality of self-esteem. In fact, self-esteem affects everything that happens to you: how you create the narrator, what plots you can attract to yourself, and how you read others.

Good self-esteem is unfakeable. You cannot successfully pretend you have it when you don't. People with reasonably good self-esteem have certain things in common. They don't create chaos and bad luck; they don't thwart themselves. Their path is straighter, so they waste less time doing, undoing, and redoing life tasks. They are less encumbered by psychic pain, wounds, and doubts. They find it easy to imagine things working out well for them. They are hopeful in a nonspecific way.

Good self-esteem is a process, not a result. Although core self-esteem is formed in childhood, one of the tasks of adult development is to build on what you've been given as a child. Your level of self-esteem is not immutable, but fluctuates. Adult self-esteem grows through experiencing passionate requited love, developing mastery, and accepting responsibility.

We are given opportunities to develop our self-esteem from situations that don't always go well initially. For example, Lindsay entered a speech tournament in school, but she procrastinated and ended up dashing off her speech at the last minute. When her turn came to speak, her lack of preparation was painfully obvious and she felt that she had made a fool of herself. Later, however, she faced down her embarrassment and entered an *ex tempore* competition, at which she spoke very well. In this way she transformed a situation that could have potentially diminished her self-esteem into one that enhanced it.

Control

The second major human motive out of which our plots grow is control. By this, I do *not* mean controlling other people. Adults strive for a feeling of control over their impulses, relationships, and environment—or at least a sense of not being out of control. As I use the term, *control* has to do with predicting outcomes and creating a sense of safety and order in our lives. It is a basic human drive because it ensures survival.

Sometimes the need for control is made evident by a desire for what is familiar—a fear of change—choosing situations that have little or no risk. Control can also come from knowledge of facts, of others, and of yourself. Control can be about not wanting to be surprised by life, and so never taking any risks.

Separation

Separation is a broadly defined concept that bears on all the areas in which human beings are alone rather than part of a relationship, family unit, or social group. It comprises all our experiences of loneliness, rejection, and abandonment, as well as the potential and actual pain that such experiences cause. Examples of separation include the developmental task of individuation, in which you achieve your own identity apart from your immediate family; the ability to leave someone; coping with someone leaving you; changing schools or moving to another city; getting a divorce, dealing with a death, and so forth. No matter how close you are to others in a family or romantic relationship, separation is involved: a recognition of, and comfort with, differences and boundaries that does not preclude intimacy. Separation is implied in all mergings.

• • •

The three motives work separately, but they also work together as a system. Self-esteem, the most pivotal of the three, ties them all together. How well you handle control and separation plays a part in building or eroding your self-esteem. If you are out of control, or handle separation poorly, your self-esteem suffers. When your actions arise out of low self-esteem, you are more fearful and less stable when it comes to controlling yourself and your environment. You will have difficulty creating and maintaining boundaries. As your self-esteem grows, control and separation issues become more manageable.

Increased control comes from paying attention to patterns and thus learning to predict and adapt. For example, you may notice that every time your girlfriend talks to her mother on the telephone, she becomes emotionally distant toward you; you learn to see that she has been pulled away from her adult role as your partner and back toward her role as child and daughter for a little while, and you realize that her temporary coolness is not animosity. Or let's say that you are initially surprised that your boss does not compliment you when you do good work. But as you see this behavior repeat, you learn not to be disappointed, and may even notice other ways in which your boss tries to recognize your efforts. We develop control by discerning patterns and thus detaching ourselves from certain outcomes. Further, as you learn better what you can and can't handle, you're able to cut your losses by limiting your emotional investment when appropriate. In this way your self-esteem both supports increased control and is strengthened by it.

The connection between separation and high self-esteem works the same way. For example, if others are repeatedly late or break dates, you can let them know that such behavior is not acceptable to you. Or perhaps you are finally able to consider leaving the safety of a comfortable, unchallenging job as choir director in the small town where you grew up to move to a bigger city where more opportunities exist for you to have the career you've always wanted in musical theater. In both cases you are able to do what serves you, even if it causes a painful separation. Making changes like this requires a certain level of self-esteem and self-confidence, but it also builds them up. The next separation issue you face will be easier to handle.

The three motives are like the warp and woof of your plots. If you pull out one thread, the entire fabric is altered because the pattern of relationships that holds it together has changed.

The Three Major Plots

Each of the three major human motives drives one of the three major plots of life. Your level of self-esteem determines your love plot. Your need and ability to be in control, or at least not out of control, motivates your mastery plot. Your ability to handle separation governs how you deal with loss in your life's plot. The relationship between each motive and its plot is that of an engine to a car. The engine drives the car, but other components of the car—the other plots and motives—must be in place or you won't get anywhere.

Self-esteem drives your love plot, but your level of self-esteem helps you to weather setbacks and rejections in your mastery plot; it affects the goals you can set for yourself and the amount of risk you can tolerate. Similarly, if your self-esteem is impaired, you will have fewer balanced ways to deal with loss. You will probably handle it too conservatively—for example, by choosing people to love who will never leave you, by staying in relationships or work situations too long, or by retreating from potential relationships too early because you dread the pain of separation that is implied later on.

Control affects the love and loss plots as well. If your need for control is too great, you may tend to choose a partner who is safe and not your peer—someone who won't challenge you or kick up a lot of dust in your life. If, on the other hand, you are comfortably self-possessed, you can resolve difficulties in relationships without power struggles, and survive the ups and downs without feeling exploited or dishonest. Your ability to handle loss includes foresight—your ability to anticipate losses (at least in part), to realize that they're inevitable, and to make room for them in your plot. You will tend to choose partners who are reliable, capable of deep commitment, and unlikely to abandon you. It is wise to identify which losses you can control and which you cannot. A certain amount of loss is inherent in life—people leave, move away, and die. You can be deeply frustrated if you try to control what cannot be controlled.

How well you handle separation affects the course of your love plot—whether, for example, in the face of a painful breakup, you remain able to keep clearly in mind what was positive about the relationship. Your ability to examine, stand up for, and live with differences between yourself and those you love, and to let them comfortably be themselves, is another important aspect of separation. Separation plays a part in your mastery plot when you are capable of doing independent work that you believe in, even when outsiders consider it unfashionable, uninteresting, or wrong-headed. You are able to strike out confidently in new directions without being hungry for reassurance.

The Sense of a Self

Although ultimately it is up to us to take charge of our stories and weave them together, realistically this cannot begin to happen until we reach a certain maturity. Unfortunately, we do not suddenly achieve maturity at a predetermined age, nor do we pass through life's stages in an orderly manner. Some people seem to be born wise, while others seem to be continually surprised by what life brings them.

Generally speaking, however, we cannot begin plotting in earnest until we have developed a sense of self. Until about our early twenties, we can have only one plot: a quest for identity. We are busy gathering raw story elements—scenes, episodes, events—from childhood, adolescence, and young adulthood. Some of these experiences will imprint us deeply and form our character in important ways; some will not. At this stage, the significance of events is still blurred because we don't yet have a vantage point from which to look back at our experiences and impose meaning on them. Later, of course, we will use these story elements—how well or poorly we did in school, the ups and downs of our relationships with friends and family—to construct the rudiments of our plot.

This does not mean that we should bide our time during the years of late adolescence and early adulthood until we reach the magic age. During this time we are free to test, act out, and try on possible selves. Take Tom's story, for example.

> My father told me that he'd pay my way through Stanford on one condition: I had to major in business administration. I agreed, because I really didn't have any other ideas about what I wanted to do, and I could never have afforded Stanford on my own. Then one semester, on a whim, I took an elective course in film making, and for the first time I was really turned on by school.
>
> Dad was furious. He actually threatened to disinherit me if I dropped the Bus. Ad. major. But I knew this was what I wanted to do. I sure as hell didn't want to work in an office all my life. So I left Stanford, enrolled at UCLA, changed my major to cinematography, and managed to pay for my courses without his help.

Eventually Tom earned his master's degree in film at UCLA. The screenplay he wrote for his master's project was made into a moderately successful movie; his next screenplay won an Oscar, and he has since directed three films. His father is now his biggest fan. Had Tom not used this time to explore another possible self, he would never have discovered his true vocation.

It takes time to acquire a self. Only after you have knocked around the world a bit, become moderately comfortable with your own sexuality, and gained confidence enough to know what you want and ask for it (or work for it) can you begin plotting your life. To merge with someone, to experience abandonment in sex, to have children, to grow spiritually, you need a self to return to. The adult self must be defined, tested, toughened, and shaped through a tempering process that cannot be hurried. When your character runs up against life, the result is your plot-making process.

Plots and Subplots

Even after we develop a clear sense of self our motivations fluctuate over time, leading us to concentrate on one plot and to treat the others as subplots. For example, in your twenties you may be more concerned with beginning your mastery plot of starting a career and doing well at it, while your love life is a subplot of random dates and social interactions.

Plots and subplots are not inherently different types of plots. Subplots, however, can deepen the main plots. For example, Richard's subplot—the need for more engagement—influenced both his mastery plot at work and his love plot at home:

I always knew that I wanted to be a doctor, and after I finished medical school, I went to work as an internist. But it didn't take me long to realize that dealing with all kinds of people and listening to their complaints day after day was not for me. I just wasn't cut out to be the kindly family doctor. I was coming home at night exhausted, and my mind was turning to mush. I still wanted to help people, but I realized that I would much rather work in research, where I could think creatively. This meant that I would have to go back to school and get more training, but I was willing to take the extra time to be satisfied in my work.

At the same time, I was feeling that my wife, Genelle, was more like my roommate than my romantic partner. Since our daughter was born, Genelle had turned from an active woman into a couch potato, and she seemed to be way more interested in the baby than she was in me. I knew we couldn't go on like this.

Richard felt overwhelmed at his job and lonely at home. But what was true about both situations was that he felt his needs were not being met. What he wanted, both at work and at home, was more engagement, and he was willing to rock the boat to make that happen.

As writing coach Anson Dibell said in her book *Plot*, the main plot and subplots entwine together like a braid: "One strand loops around to the outside, out of sight, then wraps in or under to become the central point before wrapping off for another turn." The three strands don't have to be equal in weight or importance, but you need all three to strengthen the braid.

Usually, the dominant plot in your life is the one that remains most unresolved: When am I going to fall in love? When will I have a job I really like and am good at? When will I get over my divorce? Where you are in your life determines which plot is central. When you're young, the quest for a relationship or to locate a domain of mastery may predominate. Once such a domain is located, mastery continues as an ongoing quest. We begin to experience loss as young people—leaving home, finishing school. But after middle age, loss inevitably becomes central to our plots.

Sometimes people have only one plot because their choices have closed off or truncated the others. Whom you choose to marry or what work you choose to do can make it impossible to have more than one plot. For example, a man who travels frequently on business may find it difficult to be an available parent. Or a woman who feels defined by her role as house-wife and mother may feel powerless to envision taking a de-termining role in her love relationships. Since her life lacks another plot in which she might feel some level of mastery, she overfocuses on relationships, which are her only form of vali-dation (and the riskiest source of self-esteem). Another classic example of lost plot options is the workaholic who becomes trapped in the work-mastery plot.

4

Love, Mastery, and Loss:
The Three Major Plots

The Love Plot

This is for you
it is my full heart
it is the book I meant to read you

—Leonard Cohen,
"This Is for You"

There are all kinds of love in the world: love of home and family, love of country, platonic love, spiritual love. But the type of love that drives most of our plots is the passionate love between two adults. This kind of love fills the spectrum. It may be gentle or intense, subtle or playful, a steady heartbeat or all encompassing. In the words of psychoanalyst Ethel Person, passionate love is "the most complete form of love because it is the one, above all, that allows for self-transformation and self-transcendence."

Romantic relationships have an inherently dramatic structure, full of mystery and risk: Will it last? How far can it go? Can it stand this test? Will it blow up at the next dinner date? Because of these uncertainties, romantic relationships offer plotting possibilities par excellence. We define our relationships by the stories we tell about them, and the love relationship is one big story made up of many interlocking little stories: how you met, how you decided you were right for each other, when you decided to move in together or get married, and so forth.

One of the things lovers do when they come together is to recount the stories of their past relationships, casting themselves as the betrayed, the desirable, the hurt, the abandoned, the misunderstood, and so on. As psychology professor Ernest Keen has said, "Being alone or not being alone is partly a matter of sharing with another crucial stories about life and truth."

When you see yourself as a sexual person, as a romantic lead, certain kinds of plots become possible. In fact, some aspects of the narrator's character can be revealed only in the plot of romantic love. Each relationship in which you involve yourself can present you with aspects of yourself of which you were unaware:

- "I never thought of myself as a jealous person, but when Gloria had dinner with an old lover I was anxious and angry."
- "When I was out with my wife at a party, and she openly disagreed with my point of view, I wanted to hit her."
- "I've always thought of myself as a feminist, and yet I wouldn't want to marry someone who earned less money than I do."
- "When my husband said he wanted to have some separate friendships, I felt like I did when I was five and my parents brought my new little brother home from the hospital."

These situations are ones that occur only in the context of an intimate relationship. No matter how tolerant and fair we imagine we will be with our beloved, it is only in the mirror of an intimate connection that we get to see what feelings we actually enact.

Sex is rife with opportunities for unprecedented self-knowledge; observing what sorts of people or behavior turn you on sexually can be quite surprising. Sex joins us with another's skin, fluids, smells. Sex is where we discover wordlessly what it is to be self and what it is to be other. Sexuality is literally about entering or being entered by another human being. There is no other experience remotely like it. We take off our clothes and with them go the signifiers of status and position—our self that we present to the outside world.

Every one of us possesses sexuality, yet thinking about our sexual fantasies as plots that reveal us can be uncomfortable or even scary. If you are willing to observe the narrative thread of your sexual desire, or the lack of it—of the dissonance between what you fantasize and what you do—you will most definitely learn something important about yourself. We will look at sex as a complication of the love plot more deeply in a later chapter.

Companionate love is filled with affection and friendship but devoid of erotic expression. Although legions of mental health professionals praise the virtues of companionate love, it lacks the opportunities for richness of experience and soulful knowledge that come from passionate love. Although some people would argue that they feel passionate love for God or nature, those are loves without the possibility of rejection and are therefore less risky to the self. Some people may even feel that they are incapable of passionate love. They crave distance and control, and fear the chaos that passion can bring in its wake. Passionate love doesn't call to them, and its riches do not seem worth its risks.

But romantic love has enormous power, and it can be an agent of transformation. In the best of relationships, the narrator is offered an opportunity to heal earlier wounds. Desiring someone who desires you in return enhances your self-esteem. Only passionate love offers such a rich experience of being in your body. Passionate love requires you to take more risks than companionate love, and thus offers a greater opportunity for growth and creative plotting.

Passionate love also offers the narrator the most intimate possible glimpse into the mechanics of another person's story. In passionate love relationships, people are more likely than anywhere else to tell you their most private story, the one they tell only themselves. The greater your intimacy, the greater your chance to hear it.

How Love Transforms Plots

Two kinds of plot-transforming possibilities are available to those who love passionately. One is the creation of a plot together with your beloved. Here, you get to play a central role in someone else's plot and that person in yours, creating a "we" in the present that stretches into the future. The other is the internal reordering and healing that love brings, the feeling that new things are possible and that one has found home, body and soul, with someone else.

Choosing which person we will passionately love is a plot-altering decision. Your beloved's character makeup opens some plot possibilities and closes off others. Your choice of a partner in passion carries with it the potential for healing, destruction, or stasis. Although the nature of your fundamental self is never negotiable, your choice of a person to construct a "we" plot with can bring out, or suppress, aspects of your character and your partner's. You may choose a partner, for example, who creates an atmosphere in which differences can be thrashed out, encouraging emotional honesty and trust, or one who creates a cold, judgmental climate that discourages confidences.

Our choice of a partner is both intuitive and conscious. We say "choice," but it resembles neither choosing dinner from a menu nor being struck by lightning. Many interlocking choices form the big choice. You choose with both your head and your heart. (A caveat: Apart from poorly educated women with children, whose spectrum of choices is often severely limited by their circumstances, there are no victims in long-term relationships; like finds like. When you scratch the surface of a long-term relationship, you find a dynamic that both parties are keeping alive—for example, she sleeps around, but he turns his head.)

Reflect on your past and present relationships. How has your choice of partner in your most recent love relationship opened up some plot possibilities and closed off others?

If your choice of a partner is not driven by love, it is driven by fear. You can be so afraid of passionate love and intimacy that you choose someone who will neither give it nor require it of you. For example, you may choose someone who has so many problems that your relationship is devoted to dealing only with his or her concerns, so you never have to deal with the vulnerability and intimacy of exposing your own. Surrendering to fear in love choices means that you never take the risk of feeling wholly vulnerable and alive, and you miss the deepest, most essential plot of love: it's better to have loved and lost than never to have loved at all.

Passionate love is the most supportive of internal change because it stands in dramatic contradistinction to our daily lives. For passionate love to be kept alive, both parties must truly desire to connect, to explore, and to manifest their passion. You cannot hide, nor can you hide from, character. The core self is not negotiable and cannot be revised or redescribed, but it can be healed by love.

Love and Marriage

Marriage is a highly charged relationship because it is where love, sex, control, and money all converge. If there is no agreement about power relations in a marriage, then either the weaker or the stronger partner (or both!) tends to feel resentful. The weaker member is usually the wife, who often earns less than her husband. A woman who earns no money at all may feel that her housewifely contribution isn't valued, and that only her husband gets to make decisions and have his needs met. The stronger partner, usually the husband, who has to support the family and make wise decisions, may resent his wife's complaining that he doesn't spend enough time with the kids. Similar power imbalances exist regarding sex. Sexual power in marriage belongs to the partner who desires less sex. The one who wants more sex or more contact has less power in the relationship. As author Phyllis Rose so astutely recognizes:

> Marriages go bad not when love fades . . . but when this understanding about the balance of power breaks down. . . . People who find this a chilling way to talk about one of our most treasured human bonds will object that "power struggle" is a flawed circumstance into which relationships fall when love fails. I would counter by pointing out the human tendency to invoke love at moments when we want to disguise transactions involving power.

Some marriages look successful from the outside, but are effectively empty. Such hollow marriages are a jointly created fiction, based more on the *idea* of marriage than the intimate reality of it. Here, a split exists between marriage as a major plot, defining each partner's identity to the outside world, and its true internal plot, which is an agreement to display the image of togetherness although little intimacy exists. Take Seth, for example:

Everyone said we had the perfect marriage. We had such a lovely home, two beautiful daughters who were doing well in private school, we were both therapists and even shared the same office. Nancy and I cooperated well in the kitchen. Our dinner parties overflowed with terrific food and conversation. No one ever saw us fight or have a harsh word, but that was just the problem. We were both so reserved, so polite, so functional, that there was very little happening between us—no spark. Our lives ran smoothly, but we actually weren't interested in one another.

I worked late most nights, and when I came home I usually wanted to be left alone. Nancy gave me plenty of space, but after a while I began to realize I didn't really want all that space. I wanted contact—real connection with someone I was genuinely interested in. Someone who would stand up to me, draw me out, fight with me, seduce me. All this ordered life was like death. Nancy didn't have a clue about this; she was happy with the status quo.

Such couples may take great satisfaction in presenting this fictional marriage to others. Skeptical of intimacy, they may reassure themselves that their friends' more passionate marriages are doomed because passion never lasts and love inevitably ends in boredom and congratulate themselves on their realism, good sense, and refusal to be deceived by romantic illusions. Hollow marriages like this are often more troubled than turbulent marriages, in which at least some passion exists.

Adultery, not surprisingly, has a profoundly divisive effect on the plot of marriage. Husbands or wives who engage in affairs rely heavily on compartmentalization. In her book *Adultery,* sociologist Annette Lawson points out that "adultery 'renarrativizes' lives that have come to feel empty of meaning without a sense of moving forward purposefully—lacking story." Each plot must be kept secret from the others; the mistress knows little about the family, the boss doesn't know that you're sleeping with his secretary, the husband must not find out about the lover, and so forth. (Bigamy is this plot pushed to its extreme; interestingly, there seem to be very few female bigamists.) The mechanism for this kind of compartmentalization is splitting; an adulterer splits the domestic from the erotic life.

In order to function in this compartmentalized fashion, one must communicate to others, and even to oneself, a continuous and deceptive plot. The partner who has affairs must create one plot for his spouse and another for his lover. These two plots are characterized not by what is *included* but by what facts and feelings are *excluded*.

For example, Don would tell his lover, Belinda, a consistent story of how bored and unhappy he was with his wife, how ill-suited she was for him, and how he only stayed with her because of the children. To his wife, Margaret, he said how happy he was and how much he appreciated her for giving him space to do his work and permission to be away some nights. When they were together, they had a very pleasant time.

Marriage plots can come dangerously close to writing themselves. Marriage is a plot told and retold throughout decades of songs, novels, and films—although, interestingly, most stories run to the tune of "and they lived happily ever after," omitting the details of how they did this. Many people feel that if they just get married, they've done enough. The tremendous work it takes to infuse a marriage with life and creativity is beyond them. Even for the most creative of married couples, the narrative pull of this institution is enormously powerful. Lilah and Steve's marriage is a good example.

Lilah, a talented painter, entered therapy at fifty with the expressed goal of leaving her marriage without capsizing emotionally. She wanted to move to her family's cottage in Maine and paint. Her husband Steve, a workaholic lawyer, liked having an artistic and stylish wife and a luxuriously bohemian house in Boston as props in his presentation to the world.

Lilah tended to be sweet and accommodating, first in her family of origin and later in her marriage. Her mother had been a tyrant who bullied her kind but ineffectual and alcoholic father. Lilah, ever terrified of confronting her mother, kept her head down and avoided conflict. She says:

> When I first met Steve, he seemed like a man who valued emotional communication. Unfortunately, this proved to be true only about his own feelings. He was stable, emotionally and financially, and able to make a lasting commitment. He told me that he really wanted to work on a relationship. After we got married, it didn't take me long to figure out that his words and actions didn't match. I wanted out then, but I felt it would be publicly humiliating to end the marriage so abruptly.

When she asked Steve for nurturance or affection, he would say she was "too needy." Frightened by his intractability and the possibility of being abandoned, she always backed down. When she managed to persuade him to accompany her on trips to Maine, he sulked and made negative comments about everything. He did not share in the activities that had value for her or brought her joy. However, Lilah accepted Steve's view of the marriage, believing that their problems were due to her insecurity and hypersensitivity. After fifteen years of marriage, she had come to accept that Steve had played no role in the breakdown of their relationship.

> I decided I must need therapy to improve myself. What a fool I was! My therapist helped me see how I had unconsciously identified with my father's role in my parents' marriage. Just like he did, I assumed that my own weakness was the source of our problems, and I tried to placate Steve when he went on the offensive.

Since Lilah's parents' marriage was so awful as to be unthinkable as a model, she got her ideas about marriage from the parents of her childhood friends. What Lilah remembered seeing were successful men who were regarded as good, attentive husbands because they bought their wives lovely gifts and took them on pleasant vacations. Children often idealize the marriages of their friends' parents because they see heavily edited versions of them, which they then compare favorably to their own parents' unedited behavior. Although the marriages Lilah observed may have been hollow, they at least presented a harmonious exterior. In her relationship with Steve, she had tried to emulate this idealized childhood view of marriage, without success.

Lilah further realized that she had defined confrontation as exclusively within her tyrannical mother's domain and therefore had avoided it at all costs. She learned to redescribe what it meant to communicate unpleasant feelings, and saw that it didn't have to lead to someone's annihilation. Lilah learned to articulate her needs and negotiate about them. When negotiation with Steve proved impossible, she acquired the strength and confidence to leave. She came to understand that losing herself in a relationship was too high a price to pay just to feel connected with someone.

With the help of her therapist, she told her husband that she wanted to end the marriage. She was able to hold to her position and not give in, even when he told her that her complaints were ridiculous and that she was making an enormous mistake. He tried to wear her down in the financial negotiations and to pressure her into going to a mediator who was a friend of his. Lilah, to her own surprise and vast pleasure, worked out what she was entitled to, asked for it, held her ground, and got it.

Steve was devastated at the thought of losing Lilah. He realized that she was serious, and as he thought about a life without her, it seemed very empty. She suggested they go to counseling together, and although Steve had opposed this in the past, he now agreed.

In counseling, they found that Lilah was much more important to Steve than either of them had realized. Having established that, Lilah was able to stand up for herself. They began talking about things in a way that brought them closer. The more they shared their feelings, the more they enjoyed being together. They learned to discuss their differences as just that, instead of waging a cold war.

The outcome was not a result that either of them had envisioned: they stayed together, but with some major revisions. Lilah began to spend two weeks of every month in her studio in Maine, where she began work on a series of canvases. Because she was spending so much time there, she was able to make contact with the curator of a college gallery nearby, who promised her a show. Steve was able to devote as much time to his work as he wanted without feeling guilty, and without being dragged to Maine. To their mutual surprise, they were always glad to see each other when Lilah came back to Boston, and each became more fully dimensional as a character to the other.

The Way You Do the Things You Do: The Mastery Plot

The work will teach you.

—Estonian proverb

The second major plot category, mastery, centers on things rather than people. It derives from our need and ability to be in control, or at least not out of control, of our environment—it does *not* mean control or manipulation of others. Mastery can apply to work and nonwork, vocation and avocation. It is the process of struggling with materials, skills, and ideas in order to achieve an increasing level of quality in an endeavor. Mastery gives us a greater ability to predict outcome and therefore a greater sense of control.

Mastery means working hard at something until you can do it well. Mastery comes when you learn something difficult without relying solely on your natural gifts to accomplish it. As you progress in learning new skills, you feel pride in your accomplishment; you set new goals as your increasing skill and understanding show you new challenges to surmount. For example, by age six it was clear that Philip was a brilliant pianist. But though he won every music competition he entered, he always felt vaguely dissatisfied. It was only when he left piano to take classes in dance, with the goal of becoming a choreographer, that he realized the joys that hard work could bring.

The Zen Buddhist path to enlightenment is "Chop wood, carry water": enlightenment can be found in the successful performance of the most mundane activities. Your mastery plot doesn't have to involve winning the Nobel Prize in order for it to have far-reaching effects in your life. Start small, wherever you are in your own mastery plot; learn to create a successful garden year after year, to program your computer, to cook inventively and well, to fix your own plumbing, to do the algebra that stumped you in high school, or to keep your house clean every day, not just when your mother comes to visit. All these quests and pursuits are directed toward gaining a sense of mastery.

Fitness is about mastery—not just physical mastery, but the confidence, ease, and power that come from being present in your body. Exercising is also a good way to deal with unruly or overpowering emotions. Art is a wonderful mastery plot because of its limitlessness. You never get good enough at it to attain full mastery and rest on your laurels, and because of its strong connection with the unconscious there's always more to express and tremendous satisfaction in doing so. Although the formal vocabulary of art may be limited, expression is not. Education is a more straightforward learning experience of mastery, and it may be only the prelude to a rich mastery plot of practicing what you studied. Psychotherapy can be another avenue to self-knowledge.

Hilary, a writer, began her mastery plot with dog training:

> Whenever I took my dog, Jake, to the park, I felt like a complete idiot. I called and called and called, and Jake would just give me a contemptuous look and run off. I knew that other dog owners were looking at me and asking, What is wrong with that woman? Can't she even call her own damn dog? Finally, I decided to bite the bullet and hire a dog trainer to work with me. It was a revelation. It turned out that she was training me, not Jake. After just a couple of lessons, Jake began to obey my commands. I found myself really paying attention and being present in the moment—before I had just hoped he would come back, but I had no real way to make him do it. After a month of practicing successfully with Jake, I found to my surprise that I was more confident in my writing. Instead of just hoping that the words would come out the way I wanted them to, I was actually able to marshall my concentration and shape the words the way I wanted them to read.

You can't just strong-arm yourself into mastery. The linchpin of mastery in all tasks—dog training, gardening, plumbing, and everything else—is the same: a commitment to quality. Without this commitment it is possible only to perform these tasks perfunctorily, without an evolving sense of mastery. The most important aspect of such a commitment is the understanding that mastery is a process. It means persevering through failure and rejection *and learning from them.* It means learning from experience and having the expectation that you will continue to have to learn.

Old age, like childhood, is accompanied by a diminution of the plot of mastery, but the reward of old age is wisdom. Those who have lived long and learned from their experience have a heightened understanding of themselves and others.

Work and Mastery

How you, as narrator, portray your relationship to your work is central to your plot:

- Do you feel that your identity is bound up in your work? Do you feel defined by what you do? Or do you feel that your work is just a way to pay the rent and that you are *really* something else? Do you see yourself as miscast in your work plot (for example, "I'm an actor, not a waiter")?
- How do you portray yourself in this plot—as a seeker, a journeyman, a budding entrepreneur, an indentured servant, a hired hand, an expert, a fuckup, an uninspired drudge, a hotshot?
- Do you see your work as an obstacle to or an instrument of your fulfillment?

The question of whether your identity is defined, obscured, thwarted, and so forth by your work is most pressing for the young. The youthful plot of mastery is the quest to identify one's true calling; the adult plot is the quest for mastery in that calling. Adults, especially older adults, are usually more comfortable with their own identity and less likely to feel that it can be stolen or lost in a job that is not fulfilling.

How the narrator handles and learns from ongoing challenges—the interplay of your skills, the tasks at hand, and what life sends your way—structures the mastery plot. Mastery is about accepting setbacks, mistakes, and failures as part of the quest. It's not about moving forward when the light turns green, but about what you do when it's red. You create your mastery plot not from your strengths and talents but from what you find difficult, how you handle rejections and limitations, what you do in spite of, and because of, the obstacles in your path. Steps toward mastery can be as small as searching used bookstores and libraries for a book you need for a project, or taking a life drawing class to improve your painting, or asking your boss how you could improve when there are rightful criticisms of your work performance.

This process is a quest if you are fortunate enough to be engaged in work that is creative and meaningful—some kind of soul work. The quest is defined by the commitment to quality. If your work is meaningful, more elements of mastery are present. If it is not, you must develop mastery by seeking challenges and projects outside your job—in a hobby or sport or volunteer work. Carly found her mastery plot outside her computer programming job:

> I had no idea the turn my life would take when we bought our little bungalow with its embarrassing eyesore of a yard. I had intended to put in only a low-maintenance herb garden that wouldn't take up a lot of time. As I began reading about herbs I became fascinated. Who would have known there were so many varieties of mint? I began to search for some of the beautiful rare varieties and that became another quest. I have become quite the expert and my yard is on our local herb society's tour. Now I look forward to daylight savings time because it gives me extra gardening hours.

Better to Have Loved: The Loss Plot

We are not suited to the long perspectives
Open at each instant of our lives.
They link us to our losses; worse
They show us what we have as it once was,
Blindingly undiminished, just as though
By acting differently we could have kept it so.

—Philip Larkin,
"Reference Back"

The third and perhaps the most problematic plot is that of loss. Health, beauty, memory, skill and mastery, friendship and love—all eventually leave us. Loss often brings with it feelings of abandonment and rejection. Loss is inevitable in life, and you must accept it and integrate it into your plot.

We have to contend not only with actual loss but with imagined or potential loss as well. Fear of loss is a powerful aspect of this plot, and may motivate people to try to master real or projected loss in a superficial or fraudulent way. This pseudo-mastery may involve either escape from loss or a life that is only flimsily attached to other people. But loss cannot be avoided; it is as certain as night follows day. We cannot escape the burden of loss: pain that some of those we have loved are lost to us and we to them, longing for lost time that cannot be recaptured, mourning for our waning powers, and regret for missed opportunities or poor choices that we've made. After a certain point in life—usually around forty or fifty—we deeply realize that life is not eternally regenerating. You can't just wake up and decide to have kids, or start life over again in a new city or country. Like it or not, the commitments you have already made have narrowed your plot choices. Furthermore, certain experiences have a meter on them, and when it's expired, you must move on.

Loss can occur in two ways: you can want something and not get it, or you can have something and lose it. Loss may take the form of unrequited love, losing your job, breaking up, moving away, walking out, surviving the death of a loved one, and so forth. Being able to handle loss includes being able to cause it: to leave a job, a lover, or a town when they are no longer right for you, for example. Most love songs concern loss and regret; it is a potent and universal experience. Implied loss, potential loss, and real loss are central to any attachment. They are what makes emotional involvement a risk.

The Narrator's Reaction to Loss

Loss is a painful, central, and unavoidable experience. While we can't avoid it, we do have a choice about how we read it, how we react to it, and what it means about our selves.

How you, as narrator, have *typically* responded to loss makes a statement about aspects of your inner self. Many of us experience loss as a confirmation of our unlovability. If someone leaves you, you may interpret this as proof that something is wrong with you—not with the other person or the situation itself. What makes loss a plot is this habitual, overlearned pattern of response, the story you use to explain it to yourself. You have probably never actually put this story into words or confessed it to anyone, but you as narrator have consistently experienced it as true and have used it to structure your experiences of emotional pain.

For instance, Ernesto felt that his girlfriends had left him because he wasn't good enough in some way. By telling himself this story over and over, he strongly affected his next love relationship. Even though Linda didn't fulfill many of his needs, he chose to marry her anyway because he knew that she was so emotionally needy that she would never abandon him. Ernesto's plot was now written in stone: he would never have to face losing another love relationship.

In preparing our loss plot, we unconsciously scan others to learn how dangerous they are to us: will she leave me, or won't she? Our portrayal of ourselves as unlovable is private, but consistent. It is habitual and fixed, overpracticed and over-learned. If this story remains unexamined—if you never ask, What did this particular loss mean? How did I handle it, and why? What were the assumptions behind my actions?—then the loss becomes generalized as a mistaken core belief: "Nothing lasts," "All lovers are unfaithful," "I'll never find anyone to love me as I am." You need authorial distance to look at your plot and learn to handle in an effective way the pain of being left.

One of the ways we may respond to loss is to cut off emotionally from the feelings of sadness. But this only delays the necessary period of grief until a later date. The only effective way to handle loss is to grieve—to acknowledge the emotion. Cutting off emotionally is always unsuccessful. The feelings are sealed away, but they invariably go underground, only to reappear later in a destructive form (addiction, for example). It is a fallacy to think you can avoid the pain of loss. You can end a situation, but you can't cut the feelings off. If you try, the emotion bursts forth later as an overreaction—you display emotion that's inappropriately strong compared to its ostensible cause. In fact, such inappropriate emotional outbursts are a sure sign that repressed feelings are seeking an outlet. The more intense the outburst, the less likely it is that the ostensible cause is the real cause.

When emotions are too intense or too difficult, you may be forced to admit to a vulnerability that is very painful to bear. But there is no escape from loss; it is inherent in attachment. Remember that acceptance and understanding lie on the other side of loss, and that there is no short cut.

Exercises for Chapter 4

Finding Your Love Plot

Divide your life into five-year segments from the age of your first serious love relationship (for example, twenty to twenty-five, twenty-five to thirty, and so on). Now write down your answers to the following questions about your love relationships for each five-year period:

1. What were the three most important moments in your love relationships?
2. What were your major frustrations?
3. What qualities in you were brought out in your love relationships?
4. What qualities in you remained hidden or unused in your love relationships?
5. How would your lover describe you?
6. If this period was a journey, where did it take you? Was it a detour, or perhaps even a dead end?

Looking at all your answers for all time periods, write down your answers to the following questions:

1. Do you see one or more common themes? What are they?
2. Can you weave these themes into a story about your love relationships?
3. Do you see things you'd like to do differently? What?

The Love Plot's Progress

Think about a romantic relationship that you were involved in that ended. Tell a story of love's progress, articulating the steps it took. For example:

Mild interest
Infatuation
Longing
Love
Disappointment
Frustration
Irritation
Disillusionment
Indifference

Boredom
Disgust
Anger
Hate

You don't have to include all of these, and you don't have to put them in this order. In fact, you may not even want to include any of these particular steps, but you should include at least three steps.

Narrating Your Love Plot

Using the outline of love's progress you developed in the previous exercise, write a brief story about it in the third person (refer to yourself as a character—"Henry" or "Rachel," not "I"). Now read it over and answer the following questions:

1. In a few words, how would you describe yourself as a *character* in your love plot? Seduced and abandoned? Jealous? Caring? Loving? Duped? Controlling? As someone who leaves others? Is this your view of yourself?
2. What is the *Narrator's* view of love? Does the narrator seem to think of romantic love as hopelessly tragic? As boring? As the most wonderful idea in the world? Do you share the narrator's point of view?

Thinking About Mastery

Before locating your mastery plot, think about mastery more generally.

1. Describe your proudest accomplishment.
2. Think of a very unlikely occupation for you. Describe yourself in that occupation.

3. Think of yourself as having done a wonderful job at work. What do you notice?
4. Think of yourself as having done a terrible job at work. What do you notice?

Finding Your Mastery Plot

Divide your life into five-year segments after the age of twenty (twenty to twenty-five, twenty-five to thirty, thirty to thirty-five, and so on). Reflect on your life in five-year intervals, and write down all the ways you have sought, perhaps unconsciously, to develop mastery, both in your work and in your daily life (you took a class, you apprenticed yourself, you tried to teach yourself a skill). Is there a difference in the two lists between your commitment to quality?

1. For each five-year period, make two lists—those things you tried in which you succeeded, and those in which you did not. Is there a stronger commitment to quality on the list of successful pursuits? Are there other differences in the way you pursued mastery when you were successful and when you were not?
2. List the difficulties, rejections, and limitations you have encountered in your mastery plot. What steps have you taken to handle them? Have they enhanced or diminished your mastery plot? Describe your greatest disappointment. What would you have done differently if you could live that situation over?

Finding Your Loss Plot

Divide your life into five-year segments after the age of twenty-five (twenty-five to thirty, thirty to thirty-five, thirty-five to forty, and so on). Reflect on the major losses you have had in your life and write them down in five-year intervals so that you can consider them (if you had any earlier in your life, include them as well). Write down your answers to the following questions about each major loss:

1. How did I handle that loss?
2. How can I see this loss in a different way? How can this loss serve me?
3. Look at the pattern formed by how you dealt with your losses. What do you feel this pattern says about you? That is, what are the assumptions and beliefs that underlie the way you deal with wanting something and not getting it, or having something and losing it? How have your ways of accepting loss changed as you've grown older?

5

Money, Escape, Sex, and Children: The Four Major Complications

Naturally one does not know how it happened until it is well over beginning happening.
> —Gertrude Stein, "Composition as Explanation"

Complications make your plots rich and interesting. They are the plot thickeners. Plots without complications make for dull reading. Indeed, the four major plot complications are all commonly considered desirable: money, escape, sex, and children. But because they frequently bring out unconscious, unexamined, or disavowed aspects of the narrator, these complications carry great power, for ill as well as for good. If any of these complications becomes a major plot in itself, it creates an imbalance that can capsize the narrative.

Money

How you define yourself in terms of money—how much you can generate, what you do with it, and how you regard others' financial status—affects what kind of narrator you are and what kind of plot you can create. Money is one of the areas in which the unconscious makes its presence most palpable. The narrator's attitudes about money carry unexamined beliefs: "Take care of me," "There's never enough money," "A woman is only cherished if her man supports her," "Since I earn the money, my needs are the most important." As singer Cyndi Lauper so astutely says, "Money changes everything."

Money, like any of the other plot complications, should never become a full-scale plot. If money becomes the most defining element in your plot—that is, if making money, or not having money, is all you ever think about—you have a problem. As long as it does not take over your plot, money can bring a positive influence to your life; a sense of control, validation, achievement, gratification, and security. It is very satisfying to earn money from work that you believe in and to use that money to provide for yourself and those you love. In this way, money can contribute to your mastery plot.

The Currency of Power

Money, even more than sex, is irrational, unexamined, and lied about. In Bob Dylan's phrase, "Money doesn't talk, it swears."

In our society people often feel that how much money you have accumulated defines your character. They consider money a reliable report card for how well you have done in your life, and they assume that people who possess a lot of money are free and powerful. Indeed, it is true that if you are unable to meet your own basic needs for food, shelter, and

clothing, then your plot will be dictated by survival impera-
tives. For the poor, money isn't a complication, it is the plot—
perhaps the only plot. After a certain threshold of financial
comfort is reached, however, money does not increase personal power. Being without money may mean powerlessness,
but possessing vast sums doesn't guarantee either power or security—in fact, it makes you more vulnerable because you
have so much more to protect!

Undeniably, money functions as a currency of power in relationships. For example, Rhonda's husband earned twice as
much as she did. So when someone had to stay home with
their son when he was sick, it was Rhonda who was expected
to do it.

Although money may not define relationships, it is never
unimportant. An inability to take care of yourself financially
irrevocably alters the power balance in your relationships.
When one person provides financially for another (either a
parent for a child or one spouse for the other), he or she is often buying control of the dependent person—whether such
control is desired or not. It is difficult, if not impossible, to
achieve any kind of autonomy without financial self-suffi-
ciency.

How Money Complicates
the Love Plot

Money and love are a long-married couple. Your love plot
may be complicated by a mate who doesn't earn enough
money for your tastes, or who earns more money than you
can ever hope to earn. A sudden windfall can give you the
power to leave a relationship that has grown stale, or can re-
juvenate a relationship that was exhausted by the need to
work to stay alive. Or, as Marnie discovered, money can tie
you to a situation that you don't really need.

Marnie met Howard when she was just twenty. Howard, a

building contractor, was fifteen years her senior and seemed to have his life together. She moved in with him soon after they met, and he paid for everything. After a few years, she started a catering business. It was not an overwhelming success, but it made some money. She became very comfortable with the lifestyle she and Howard inhabited, even though they were heavily in debt to his family for the down payment on their home and to the bank for the second mortgage on their house.

In her mid-thirties, Marnie began to hear her biological clock ticking loudly. Howard, approaching fifty, was not enamored of the idea of parenthood. Marnie realized that she was no longer in love with Howard, and in fact barely wanted to spend any time with him. She wanted to leave him and get on with her life, but was afraid that she would not be able to support herself or find someone who could both give her a child and support her.

When you think about how money has complicated your love plot, has it been a positive complication or a negative complication, as it was for Marnie? Sometimes we become settled in a comfortable lifestyle brought about by two incomes, and we let our fear of losing that comfort eclipse the question of whether we are happy with our choice of mate.

How Money Complicates the Mastery Plot

Money, of course, can be a wonderful reward for mastery; for some people, it's a goal. But it can also be a powerful complication. For example, you may have achieved a high degree of mastery in a field that will never pay you enough money, or you may be chasing money at the risk of never achieving mastery. And money can complicate the mastery plot in ways we can't anticipate.

Warren, a landscape architect and garden designer, loved

the challenge of creating a garden for each client's needs: the house, the plot of land, the desire and ability to maintain the garden, the plant preferences. He learned a lot about people from their homes and gardens, and was full of pride when his clients were pleased. After he and his wife had their second child, he was hired to do the garden of the head of a computer company. It was an extremely large home and Warren did an austere but effective job. The client offered him a full-time job landscaping and maintaining the grounds of the computer company's headquarters for twice his current yearly income. Warren accepted the job, but soon found that, without human contact or any variety to the plant selection, his work had become drudgery.

How Money Complicates the Loss Plot

Money can't buy happiness, but it can seem to, and that's the primary way in which it can complicate the loss plot. Out-of-control spending or money hoarding usually has to do with feelings of grief and sadness that have not been expressed.

For example, Ed and Brian had been together for twenty years. After Brian died, Ed's friends became very worried about him. He went on a shopping binge that lasted for months. First he went on a trip to Hawaii and stayed at the most deluxe hotel. When he returned he ate out at fancy restaurants and bought lots of new clothes. The constant consuming allowed Ed to avoid dwelling on the loss of Brian—until the collection agencies started calling.

Escape

You can find escape in any pursuit that allows you to forget yourself. Escape can be wonderful and productive: you can escape your terrible day at work by getting up from your desk and taking a walk around town. You can escape from your boring apartment by painting it in bright new colors. You can escape your worries by taking some time out to meditate or get a massage.

But you can also opt for a negative escape: you can run up a huge credit card bill to escape the fact that you have no cash. You can drink yourself into oblivion every day at five to escape the fact that you hate your boss. You can fall into the arms of a lover to escape the problems you face with your spouse.

Escape from self-consciousness and self-observation, and from stress or misfortune, can be both good and necessary, but escape from your feelings is neither—and in the long term it is impossible. As painfully raw or terrifying in their intensity as they may be, your feelings are yours. There is no escape from them, only temporary distraction. Feelings that are denied wait and come back, often in a disguised or compounded form that's much more difficult to address. For example:

- Linda pretended that she wasn't upset when her husband said she was overweight, but for the next few weeks she found it difficult to stay sober.
- Ralph was becoming increasingly uncertain if he could do all the work his new promotion required and also deal with his demanding and critical new boss. Instead of raising these objections at work, he went home each night and yelled at his son for anything less than perfect academic performance.

When escape becomes a full-blown plot rather than a complication, you are in serious trouble. Substance abuse, eating disorders, and workaholism are examples of plots of escape. When escape becomes a plot, two other major plots, love and mastery, are in danger of being annihilated.

How Escape Complicates
the Love Plot

Escape can easily capsize the love plot entirely. In love relationships the conflict and differences couples seek to escape catch up with them sooner or later. All love relationships have conflicts—it's whether and how you deal with them that makes the difference. If one or both partners are trying to escape anger or difficult feelings, they will show up in a more volatile form in a different time and place—usually, in bed.

For example, Bob was terrified of conflict and confrontation. Usually he just agreed with people to their face and then went on to do as he pleased. His wife, Elaine, grew more and more upset as she tried to bring up things about the relationship that were bothering her. Bob would avoid Elaine by escaping further into his work—working longer hours and going on more frequent business trips. With Bob around so infrequently, Elaine tried to concentrate on the positive. After a while, she stopped bringing up things that bothered her, and Bob stopped working such long hours. Then the cycle would start up again, with Elaine complaining and Bob avoiding conflict and creating distance, each cycle growing in intensity and despair.

How Escape Complicates
the Mastery Plot

The consequences of escape, when it gets out of hand and becomes too important—that is, when it becomes its own plot—are passivity, loss of control, and loss of freedom. You forfeit the ability to write and direct your own plot because the escape plot doesn't need an author. It is powerful, rigid, and repetitive in structure. Addiction is a very good example of an escape plot. When we crave oblivion or chemical enhancement of reality because it seems unsatisfactory on its own, we lose the opportunity to affect that reality on our own behalf.

The emotions that are uncomfortable enough to prompt us to escape have to be acknowledged and felt before they will go away. Sometimes the emotions are hard to identify, and they may be masked by boredom or depression; but if we look deeply enough, we can always find them. Forgetfulness and ease are enormously seductive, but we must ask: What is it that we want so badly to forget?

For example, Bruce, the bright son of a famous and ruthless trial lawyer, was "bored" by his work as an attorney. On weekends, he would go to a resort and gamble all day and night. Soon he was deeply in debt and unable to concentrate on his legal work. In therapy, he realized he had become addicted to gambling as a way of escaping his complicated and competitive feelings with his father.

On the other hand, escape is restorative unless it is misused. It offers a chance to switch off, have fun, and recharge your batteries. Everyone needs pleasure, nonproductive and nonresponsible activity—play! Further, play is the source of creativity. Psychoanalyst D. W. Winnicott suggests that there are two general attitudes toward life: creativity and compliance. A creative attitude, he says, gives us the feeling "that living is worth living," while compliance carries the idea that "nothing matters."

Many people have the unfortunate and mistaken belief that if they can't draw a picture or write a novel, they're not creative. In fact, we evince creativity in many ways—how we solve problems, put together a photograph album, decorate a room, invent a costume, plan a garden, and, of course, how we write and rewrite our life plots.

It is important to understand that escape does not mean simply controlling our impulses to do things that are bad for us, but finding joy in positive escapes. Our mastery plot also affords us positive opportunities to escape when we couple our skill at something we enjoy with a sense of play. Winnicott states, "It is in playing and only in playing that the individual child or adult is able to be creative and to use the whole personality, and it is only in being creative that the individual discovers the self."

How Escape Complicates the Loss Plot

Mourning is the opposite of escape because it meets the pain of loss head-on, acknowledging and confronting the magnitude of the loss and the intensity of the emotion, rather than disguising the pain or escaping from it. (Of course, some losses, such as a traumatic death, incest, or being victimized by a violent crime, are too overwhelming to face all at once; they must be mourned slowly, so that the pain is not incapacitating.) Those who cannot mourn want a respite, and may choose to escape through promiscuous sex, drug and alcohol abuse, and so forth. Productive escape is possible, too; some people read novels, exercise, garden, make art, or polish the kitchen floor until it could substitute for a dining-room table.

As we have seen, each of us can play more than one role— not just in our own plots but in others', too. Having more than one role to fall back on can protect you from feelings of inadequacy, failure, desolation, and guilt when things go wrong. For example, Lulu, a travel agent, was married, had a three-year-old daughter, and ran in marathons all over the country. When chronic knee problems forced her to give up running, she found the loss easier to accept because she could both comfort herself with her success in other realms and also concentrate more on those other roles as she was letting go of running for good. We long for escape when we have to deal with an extremely painful or scary situation. If you have invested yourself only in one role and it goes badly, that can be devastating. If, however, you play many different satisfying roles, it is possible to protect yourself by shifting where you focus your attention.

Suicide is the ultimate escape plot, the one that obliterates the possibility of future revision. It also leaves everyone your life has touched with a major rewrite on their hands.

Sex

Sex is the best-known plot complication. It has driven the plots of the finest dramas and the worst trash for thousands of years, from Greek drama to Shakespeare to TV miniseries. That this should be so is not surprising. Sex is the first power, the generative power, the juice that makes the world flow. As Sallie Tisdale, author of *Talk Dirty to Me,* has written, "There is peace in the chaos of sex because it is one place we can find each other in ourselves and ourselves in each other."

Although sexuality is one aspect of being that everyone shares, each person contends with sexual feelings in a particular way. Everyone must deal with his or her sexual self. Since sexuality is not a rational enterprise, it is often the wild card in the deck, having the power to enter the other suits and wreak havoc. Real passion is volatile. It has the power to unleash chaos. When you are a wholly sexual being, completely in that experience, you lose the burden of self-consciousness. Oblivion and an obliteration of the self-observer are the hallmarks of a wholly compelling sexuality.

In our sexual self we find our most profound isolation: we know only our own experience, and not even very much about that because it is so enmeshed in our deepest dreams and delusions. As with money, we are too vulnerable to its power to be honest about it. People want to present a desirable sexual self without appearing vulnerable.

Of all our plots, we edit those involving sex the most thoroughly. In telling our sexual stories, for example, we tend to portray ourselves as more desirable, more satisfied, more normal—whatever that is!—than is true, or we don't discuss it at all. Often, people tell their friends about their infidelities only when the relationship is over. Not surprisingly, the famous and celebrated frequently present us with persons who are very different from the reality of their sexual nature and choice of partners. The conservative, straight-arrow FBI head J. Edgar Hoover was apparently a homosexual who liked to don a tutu; John F. Kennedy, whose marriage to Jackie was at one time considered a fairy-tale romance, had numerous affairs and one-night stands.

People often lie about themselves when it comes to sex because they fear that the truth is too exposing, socially unacceptable, or politically incorrect. (In some cases, they might be right; to tell the truth can be a risk, for example, if public knowledge about your sexual preferences would endanger your career.) They wonder if they are bad, perverted, weird, insatiable.

We know little about our own sexuality because the emotions involved are so powerful that we resist looking at them. Desire makes us incredibly vulnerable. Desire is the sexual emotion—it is a real feeling, like fear and joy, and is not to be confused with simple physical lust. Passionate love and carnal lust are not the same thing. Carnal lust, however thrilling, is doomed to be short-lived. Since the only real connection it makes is sexual, it deals with only a part of the other person. Passionate love, however, includes carnal lust along with a deep and soulful knowledge of the beloved.

In seduction, people often act in ways that they think will be regarded as sexy. Real passion is combustion—social and personal dynamite. It sweeps you along like a tidal wave, revealing unsuspected aspects of your self (avidity, compliance, wildness, relentlessness, domination). Truly passionate sex is always mutual—if you are pursuing someone who is not sexually available, the true text is loss.

Since sex frequently slips out of control, social and religious authorities have traditionally tried to govern it, portraying it as bad or dangerous. In recent years the media have taken this control further by linking sex to violence in a cause-and-effect relationship. Movies that carry this message are numerous. In *Basic Instinct,* a man is fascinated by a sexually liberated woman and ends up being stabbed with an ice pick. In *Fatal Attraction,* a man who loves his wife has a brief affair that turns murderous. In *Sea of Love,* a man contacts women through personals ads and murder follows. The repeated message is: be sexual and violence will follow.

Sex is one of the most powerful forces we encounter in our lives. It is the rich essence of life itself. As such, it can be the oil that makes our plot run smoothly and creatively forward. It becomes a complication when we pretend sexually—when we pretend to be virginal when we are really turned on, when we pretend to be brutally macho when we are really hurting inside, when we pretend to be in love with our spouses and hide our love affairs—or when we are genuinely out of touch with our sexual selves.

Sexual Fantasy

Sex offers us a way to get to know ourselves that is unlike any other. Sexual fantasies, if we pay attention to them, reveal character in a way that nothing else touches. Sallie Tisdale describes how sexual fantasy reveals one to oneself:

> What I *do* is the product of many factors, not all of them sexually motivated. But what I imagine doing is pure—pure in the sense that the images come wholly from within, from the soil of the subconscious. The land of fantasy is the land of the not-done and the wished-for. There are private lessons there, things for me to learn, all alone, about myself.

These "private lessons" are about one's core sexual nature, which if unexamined can lead to some very messy plot complications. The discrepancy between our style of sexual fan-

tasy and our actual lovemaking reveals the essence of a certain part of our character: what we like to do, what we like
done to us, what we would only fantasize about but would
never want to happen, how we want others to perceive our
sexual self. A big gap between fantasy and reality can be a
road map to certain uncomfortable and disavowed aspects of
the narrator. For example, if you are turned on by the idea of
being tied up but pretend you like sex only in the missionary
position, it may be a sign that you have some unexplored issues to look at.

Our sexual fantasies give us information about ourselves in
the same way that our dreams do: we gravitate toward fantasies that produce or satisfy a state of desire. For example,
Barbara's sexual fantasies when she masturbated were often
about having sex with more than one man or being naked and
sexually aroused with more than one man watching. When
she reflected on them, she knew it was not something she ever
wanted to act out or even share with someone. Her fantasies
were about being a sex goddess, an object of desire for men in
general. In these fantasies, Barbara felt free and flawlessly
beautiful and desirable—the burden of self-consciousness was
lifted. She could accept the emotional content of her fantasies
without feeling uncomfortable or driven to actually enact
them.

For a sexual fantasy to work—that is, to turn you on—you
must enter it and give yourself over to it. Unlike actual sex,
where you can be physically present but otherwise composing
your list of errands for the day, fantasy requires your complete
attention to be effective and enveloping.

How Sex Complicates
the Love Plot

Most of us can give an example, from our own lives or the
lives of others, of how sex can complicate the love plot: an af-

fair can break up a marriage, bad sex can terminate an otherwise blissful relationship, a man who prefers virginal women
may reject the woman he loves because he discovers she has
had other sexual partners. The list goes on and on. The following story illustrates how sex can complicate the plot of
companionate love:

Christie had been in a companionate marriage with Ted for
five years. They made love once a week or so, and that seemed
to be fine for both of them. In fact, Christie had always
thought people made too much fuss about sex. Her love plot
was clicking along on this track until sex suddenly derailed it:

> I volunteered at my daughter's preschool two afternoons a
> week, and so did Ben. He was divorced and his wife had cus-
> tody, and spending time with his son at preschool was incred-
> ibly important to him. I had known him casually for a year,
> and he was just another nice Dad. But one day as we were
> both helping with an art project, I suddenly became aware of
> him—with paint and glue all over his shirt—and how attrac-
> tive he was. I guess he was attracted to me too, because one
> afternoon he complimented me on my earrings and gave me a
> ride home. I was stunned to find myself fantasizing about
> him—I pictured us having sex in the back of his pickup truck,
> for God's sake! I was pretty obsessed with him, and I started
> taking special care with my appearance when I knew I would
> see him at school.
>
> Inevitably, we made love, and to say that it was a mind-
> blowing experience would be an understatement. I truly hadn't
> understood that this was what all the fuss was about. A door
> seemed to open inside me, and I suddenly saw my marriage
> very clearly: Ted was always overwhelmed and depressed with
> work, and he took very little interest in me as a woman. It was
> probably obvious to all my friends, but I just hadn't realized it
> until I began to spend more time with Ben and found myself
> longing for him in ways that were unfamiliar and exciting.
>
> Now my juices were flowing. I began to feel more con-

nected to my body than I had in years. I started going to the gym more often, and I bought new clothes to make my body happy. I was much more alive sensually than I ever believed I could be. I couldn't hide these changes, and at base I didn't want to. Ted sensed that I had changed, although it was months before I told him about Ben. I'm not sure what I'm going to do about my marriage: my new self-knowledge has changed me, and I don't want to go back to the old me even if Ted and I break up.

Eventually, Christie and Ben stopped seeing each other. But she couldn't continue in her comradely marriage to Ted, either: Her long unknown sexual self was no longer containable.

How Sex Complicates the Mastery Plot

Sexual activities that are wildly out of sync with the rest of our lives can destroy our mastery plot in an instant. Gil, for example, had spent twenty-five years building up a legal career with a strong commitment to public service. He had a solid marriage, and three children in whose lives he took an active interest. For years his friends had begged him to run for head of the school board, and finally he agreed. He was very excited about the possibilities the job seemed to offer.

Unfortunately, Gil had also spent the last twenty-five years crudely coming on to every young woman he encountered, despite being continually rebuffed by them. These women had built up genuine and strong anger toward him over the years, but when his actions went unpunished by the firm despite their complaints, they were unwilling to go public. When election time drew closer, however, things suddenly changed. A young intern working at the firm sued Gil for sexual harassment. Her action encouraged other women to come forward as well, and soon Gil's political career was finished.

Sex does not necessarily have to complicate mastery in a negative way, however. Its power can be tremendously generative. Henry Miller used his love affair with his wife, June, as material for his greatest books, transforming his obsession with her into art. After a particularly abysmal period of depression, when he stayed in bed for ten days, Miller had a revelation: instead of actually killing himself, he could write about it. According to Louise De Salvo in *Conceived with Malice,* "He could incorporate his personal pain into a work of art that would be 'something greater than the frame of personal misfortune.'"

Sex and Loss

People who pursue lovers who are unavailable are as common in real life as they are in literature and popular entertainment. The text of those complex couplings is loss, not intimacy. For example, Diane, a single woman in her thirties, fell in love with Hal, a married coworker. He told her that he would never leave his wife, but she chose not to believe him.

> How could he say he wouldn't leave his wife? We had the most incredible sex! What he had with his wife couldn't possibly be as good. But he always left my bed at night to go back to her. He spent the weekends and holidays with her too, and I was always alone. I hadn't minded being alone before I met him, but being alone and knowing he was with his wife was hell.

Angry, depressed, and fed up, Diane finally ended the affair. A year later, after dating several available men, she again became passionately involved with a married man. Just as Hal had done, he left her at night and spent weekends and holidays with his wife. She spent long evenings and weekends alone.

I felt abandoned. One night as I sat in my apartment with nothing but the television to keep me company, I began to wonder why I kept getting left. You know, "Why does this always happen to me?" I felt the same way as a child—I was born fifteen years after my brother, an accident. My parents never really wanted me, and I grew up feeling pretty abandoned. Suddenly the lightbulb went on over my head, just like in a cartoon. I realized that I was drawn toward men who would leave me—it was a state I was comfortable with, in some awful way.

When Diane discovered that she was involving herself in sexual situations that would reenact her painful feelings of loss over and over, she decided enough was enough. She decided to get some therapy to help her to deal with her earlier feelings of loss directly.

Children

Children—wanted and unwanted, infants and adults—can really play havoc with your life plot. Our attitudes toward them, and their attitudes toward us, can complicate everything that once seemed so simple.

Theoretically, parents and children can provide one another with unconditional love that isn't available from friends and lovers. In the best of circumstances, this can be a wonderful, nurturing fountain of solace in an uncertain world. Unfortunately, the best is not always available. We sometimes look to our children, or are looked to by our parents, as sources for the unconditional love that isn't there romantically. In many marriages, parents have a better relationship with their children than they do with each other, and this can be as destructive for the child as it is for the marriage. Fay Weldon described this situation succinctly in her novel *Remember Me:*

Hilary, thinks Madeleine. Hilary, my child. What will become of Hilary? What have I been thinking of, these years, these times? Thinking myself Jarvis's wife, when all I was was Hilary's mother? What have I done to Hilary?

Undeniably, one of the great rewards of having children is the occasion to receive the solace and healing of unconditional love from your child. Furthermore, by having children, *you* are given the opportunity to love unconditionally, which is healing and restorative as well. Remember, however, that children are loaned to you. You get to be central in their plot only for a while. Being a parent is an episode, albeit a long one, in your life. When it comes to an end, which it always does, you are thrown back upon yourself as both the author and central character of your own plot.

Being a Parent

The present generation of parents, the baby boomers, try to do parenting in a more self-conscious way than their predecessors. Since they have come of age in a psychologically oriented culture, they have examined the various flaws in their parents' methods. After looking at what went wrong, they often strive to do it differently.

Until recently, being a father was not a significant male plot complication. The *idea* of fatherhood was important, but the *activity* of fatherhood wasn't. There really was no established story for fatherhood: for men, any time spent with their children was considered laudable. Today, however, much of that seems to have changed. Fathers are finding their own plots. Ben remembers:

When my wife and I were divorced, I was devastated. My son Dylan was everything to me. That we couldn't live together anymore was unthinkable. Before I had a child, I was Ben. But after I had a child, I was Ben, Dylan's dad. Spending time with

Dylan at preschool was a revelation for me about myself: I loved being there, I loved watching him play with the other kids, learning about who he was and how he moved in the world. I learned things about myself I never knew were there.

You don't have to be a natural father to experience the kinds of changes children bring to your life. Mitchell had studied theater in Europe in his twenties, and had traveled around the world for years giving acting classes and performing. He had had many relationships, but had never married. Now, at fifty, he managed an avant-garde theater company in Manhattan, and his life was going well. One day Mitchell got a letter informing him that his cousin, a single mother, had committed suicide, leaving her ten-year-old son, Adam. Adam had nowhere else to go: no one knew who his father was, and his grandparents were long dead. It was either live with Mitchell or be put in a foster home, so Mitchell, with some trepidation, took him in.

Although Mitchell's freedom was reduced immediately and dramatically, he was surprised to find his love for Adam growing and growing. He let Adam share his life: He helped Adam with his homework as they sat at Mitchell's favorite cafe, and he gave Adam a job helping with props so that they could spend time around each other even when Mitchell had to work. The two supported and nurtured each other in ways that took them both by surprise.

While fathers are now more free to determine their parenting plots, most women measure themselves against the time-honored child-rearing plot that harks back to a time when women didn't work outside their homes and were able to greet their children every day after school with freshly baked cookies; provide rides to sports practice, lessons, or play dates; and help with homework. Today, however, most mothers find themselves falling short of this ideal because the reality of life, or their own desire, compels them to work outside the home.

For example, Trisha, a corporate attorney, wondered why she ever believed in the fiction that she could "have it all." She went to work at 6:30 A.M. so that she could come home in time to drive Miranda to her piano lessons and dance class. One afternoon a week she baked brownies with her daughter or thought up some other "meaningful" activity for them to do. After dinner, Trisha prepared briefs for her clients. But when helping Miranda with her homework began to cut into her evenings, Trisha realized that she couldn't keep up the pace. She arranged for someone else to take Miranda to her lessons so that she could get her work done, but she was wracked by guilt.

The Family That Never Existed

One obstacle to seeing our plots clearly is strong nostalgia for a plot of family that may never have existed. Nuclear families as portrayed on television sitcoms seem to embody these wished-for families. The show most frequently mentioned by my female clients as the ideal that they compared themselves to (and fell short of) was *The Donna Reed Show*. The image of Donna, always cool, dry, and concerned in her starched shirtwaist dresses, pearls, and high heels, torments them to this day.

Consider the opinions of two experts on the family. The first, research psychologist Arlene Skolnick, points out how current ideas about the decline of "family values" are based on idealized notions of a nonexistent past: "Whether the golden age [of family life] is located in the 1950s, the Victorian era, or the preindustrial past, its portrayal in these writings bears approximately the same relation to the historical record as a Disneyland setting bears to its historical counterpart."

Stephanie Coontz, who has written extensively on family history, describes the effects of such myths on families: "The most common reaction to a discordance between myth and reality is guilt. Even as children, my students and colleagues tell me, they felt guilty because their families did not act like those on television. Perhaps the second most common reaction is anger—a sense of betrayal or rage when you or your family cannot live as the myths suggest you should be able to do."

Children are often thought to confer adulthood and are sometimes displayed like badges of legitimacy to show the outside world. Like parents on TV sitcoms, having children endows us with seriousness and power: "I'm a Dad and I know what's best for you." "It's that way because I say so." Parents are the center of their children's world, and children believe they have the answers. (The truth, however, is that parents have only *episodes* when they know the answers.)

Although people with children often cling tenaciously to marriage no matter how bad it is, divorce can function as either a negative or a positive plot element. Staying in a marriage is often taken to mean that the relationship is "working," and divorce that it's "not working," although these generalities may mask quite different realities. Traditional wisdom has held that an intact family is always better for the children than a "broken home," but Arlene Skolnick contests this widely held view:

> There is increasing evidence that parental conflict, whether in the form of shouting or hitting or cold hostility, which may exist in both intact and divorcing families, is a key factor in children's psychological well-being. Yet studies of the effects of divorce rarely compare divorced families to intact families with high levels of conflict. . . . If we care about children, we need to focus less on the form of families they live in and more on ways of supporting their well-being in all kinds of families. We need to accept the fact that while the family is here to stay, so are divorce, working mothers, and single-parent families.

Divorce is never easy for children, but the how of it is more important than the what. A bad marriage can be worse for children than a divorce. When children are living in a conflict-ridden, hostile, or emotionally dead atmosphere, divorce can be a positive plot element. What we need are new plots for the successful postdivorce family, in which children thrive and maintain good relationships with both parents.

If your kids don't see you having a life, falling down and getting up again, they have no model of real life to learn from. As one single mother told me, "I couldn't show my daughter Betty Crocker, because Betty Crocker didn't live here anymore. But she got to see me being upset, and being more upset, and getting over it, and moving on."

How Children Complicate the Marriage Subplot

Marriage's public face and its internal workings may be vastly different. One thing is certain, however—every marriage is a story. In fact, it is at least four stories: his, hers, "ours," and the public's.

Children see yet another story because they view their parents' marriage from a unique vantage point. They see the unacknowledged story of how things *really* work at home and who has power over what—for example, Dad bullies Mom and she covers it up to her friends, or Mom is nice to Dad in public but contemptuous at home. Children notice if what is presented to the outside world is radically and frequently different from what is experienced at home. Observing the mismatch between words and behavior, they learn that the truth is always revealed by behavior. Further, they learn that when description and experience differ, experience must be kept a secret. Here's Brenda's story:

> I remember spending night after night at the dinner table listening to my mother yell at my dad, telling him how stupid he was, how he always bungled situations at work. Dad would just hang his head in shame and defeat. I know he hated being dis-

respected like that in front of us kids. I couldn't understand how she could do that to him, and why she hated him so much. Then I would hang around my mom's card games and listen to the way she described Dad to her friends. She was glowing! She bragged about how successful he was in business, and how good he was at handling people. I learned the meaning of hypocrisy at an early age.

Parents tend to focus too intensely on their children when something crucial is missing from the marriage—when the parents are not meeting each others' needs and are not central, in a positive way, to each other's plots. Because of the lack of real intimacy between the parents, the child is thrust into the foreground and becomes too important a player in the parents' marriage plot. In this scenario, the child is the main project they share, and their own connection becomes secondary. However, children want and need to be minor characters in their parents' marriage plot. They can't carry the weight of the marriage; when forced to play a bigger role, they sacrifice some of their capacity to play, experiment, and learn in order to assume the burden. Their importance brings power, but it is a false kind of power—false because it is unfairly awarded, unprepared for, and produced by a fraudulent bargain between the parents.

For example, Renee and Raymond were utterly focused on their son, Cody. If he had a bad day at school or someone picked on him, it was a tragedy. His eating and sleeping habits were the topic of endless discussion. In fact, Renee and Raymond got along best when they were talking about Cody. But at other times, they had very little in common. They had drifted apart as a couple, and worrying about Cody was the only way they had to reconnect.

Having children irreversibly complicates the marriage plot. After a couple has children, the number and frequency of household tasks escalate. Who does them? You cannot just skip a feeding, or decide to change the baby's diaper next week. Children's needs are enormous, pressing, and immediate. Arlie Hochschild entitled her book on this subject *The Second Shift*, referring to the child-related jobs parents must do before they go to work and after they return home. One typical arrangement was reported to her by the Holts, who have a small child:

> One day, when I asked Nancy to tell me who did which tasks from a long list of household chores, she interrupted me with a broad wave of her hand and said, "I do the upstairs, Evan does the downstairs." What does that mean, I asked. Matter-of-factly, she explained that the upstairs included the living room, the dining room, the kitchen, two bedrooms, and two baths. The downstairs means the garage, a place for storage and hobbies—Evan's hobbies. She explained this as a "sharing" arrangement, without humor or irony—just as Evan did later. Both said they had agreed it was the best solution to their dispute. Evan would take care of the car, the garage, and Max, the family dog. As Nancy explained, "The dog is all Evan's problem. I don't have to deal with the dog." Nancy took care of the rest.

"The rest" included all the care required by their child. This "upstairs-downstairs" arrangement leans heavily on fraudulent redescription as a plotting device. The euphemistic division of labor allowed Nancy to stay in her exploitive marriage without losing her last shred of self-esteem. The price, however, for fraudulent redescription is living with lies, which takes an emotional toll and renders authentic intimacy impossible (the Holts' marriage suffered gravely as a result).

Hochschild, however, did see some couples who were able to divide the labor more equitably, so that both were satisfied. These men and women "did not load the former role of housewife-mother onto the woman, and did not devalue it as one would a bygone peasant way of life. They shared that role between them. What couples called "good communication" often meant that they were good at saying thanks for one tiny form or another of taking care of the family."

The Precious Child

Another undesirable plot possibility is the development of the "superbaby": the overindulged, overscheduled, overly precious child. In this plot, indulging is another job on top of ensuring the child's basic needs. In any standoff between the parents' needs and the child's, the child's will prevail, reducing the parents to mere props.

This is a particular hazard for baby boomers, many of whom grew up privileged and experienced the power of seeing their wishes and hopes enacted in the culture. They easily lose the point of view of the adult—their childhood self is often so primary that they are unable to integrate the adult's needs with those of the child.

This was certainly true for Trisha, the attorney, who found herself unable to handle the schedule she had set up for Miranda. She had a deep-seated belief that it would be a great tragedy if her daughter did not have the dancing lessons and the piano lessons that she herself had enjoyed. Unfortunately, Trisha never consulted Miranda about her own desires. If she had, she would have discovered that Miranda hated practicing, and was in fact developing an active dislike for classical music. Worse, she was embarrassed by her developing body and found getting into a leotard for ballet practice to be torture beyond belief. She never shared these feelings with her mother, however, because Trisha was so clearly sacrificing her own life to give her these "gifts."

The Prop Child

Trisha has come perilously close to treating Miranda as a prop or, even worse, as a trophy in her own plot. Sadly, instead of treating children as separate people, parents sometimes see them as report cards on their own lives.

Having a child is a public act and provokes from others

strong assessments of you as a parent and ultimately as a person. "My son the doctor" sounds better to others than "my son the carpenter." People feel that others will judge them on the basis of their child's looks, achievements, amount of body fat, and so on. This is an updated version of the old notion of living through your children. But when children are seen as a reflection of your success or failure, they are not allowed to make their own mistakes, get fat, have pimples, or earn poor grades, for example, because they are props in *your* plot and you don't want those elements in your story. (You should, of course, be genuinely concerned for your child's welfare, but such concern is informed by a different motivation.) There are limits to your control over other people, an issue we will discuss at greater depth in a later chapter.

How Children Complicate the Love Plot

Children can complicate your love plot if you use them as a way of creating distance between yourself and your mate, or if you use them and their needs as an indirect way to communicate your own needs to your mate.

For example, George shared a joint custody arrangement with his ex-wife, under which he had their daughter, Elizabeth, half the week. During the year since the separation, he had put a lot of time into Elizabeth—taking her to the movies, playing games with her, fixing her special dinners. Out of a mix of love and guilt, he found it almost impossible to say no to her. Quite suddenly, he fell in love with a woman named Rosa, whom he met through a friend. But Elizabeth had grown used to being the center of her father's attention, and when his daughter was around, George focused exclusively on her. He insisted that they do whatever Elizabeth preferred. When Rosa finally suggested that this arrangement was difficult for her and probably unhealthy for Elizabeth, George behaved defensively and broke off their romance. George used his inability to set limits with his daughter as a way of creating distance with his girlfriend.

How Children Complicate
the Mastery Plot

Children can complicate the mastery plot if you use their needs as an excuse for not addressing your own mastery needs. If, for example, you have fears about taking a class or taking other steps to be more in the world, you could simply say, "My kids need me," stay home, and later resent them for it. Of course, every decent parent makes some professional sacrifices to carve out time for children, but that is different from hiding behind your role as a parent to avoid facing your fears.

Virginia, a freelance writer and editor, worried what would happen to her career after divorce left her the sole caretaker for six-year-old Max. As it turned out, it was the best thing that could have happened to her work life. Before, with the security of a double income, she had always procrastinated and let little upsets get in the way of her productivity. Now, however, with Max really depending on her, she was able to raise her rates, budget her time, and not give in to her negative emotions. Her editing and writing business began to thrive as a result of her new ability to manage her time and emotional life effectively.

How Children Complicate
the Loss Plot

Sometimes we use children to replace what we have lost. For example, Simone and her sister, Carol, had been very close all their lives. They shared everything as children, were roommates throughout college, and even after both were married they talked on the phone every day. When Carol died suddenly at age twenty-five of a brain aneurysm, Simone fell apart. She felt a hole inside so big that nothing could fill it. She was unable to work and became completely dependent on her husband, Gary. After a year of mourning, she was still sad but she began to get her life back together. She no longer thought of Carol every minute and was able to resume her career as a decorator.

Suddenly, the idea came to her that she wanted to have a child, even though she and Gary had expressly agreed that they would not have children. Without telling him, she stopped using birth control. Within three months she was pregnant, and nine months later she had a baby girl that she named Carol.

Without realizing it, Simone was seeking to replace the closeness she felt with her sister with a new person of her own creation. The danger was that she would always see the baby not as a person in her own right but as a replacement for her sister. And although Gary found that he loved his daughter, he was angry at Simone for not including him in her decision and concerned about her obsession with the baby.

Exercises for Chapter 5

How Money Complicates Your Plots

1. Imagine you won $20 million in the lottery. Write a few lines about how it changed your life. How did you feel about it? Did it change your relationships with people? Did you quit your job?

2. Imagine that you are transported to a world that doesn't use money. Write a few lines about how this changes your life. Do you miss money, or are you relieved? What do you do for fun?

3. Write a paragraph describing how money worked in

your childhood. Did you get an allowance? Did you have to work for money? Were your parents "rich" or "poor"? Now write a paragraph describing how money works for you today. How do your two paragraphs relate to each other?

4. Now that you have a handle on the money issue, think about how money has complicated your love, mastery, or loss plot (for example, the job you took because of the huge salary, the person you broke up with because he or she had no financial future, the time your dad lost all his money in a bad stock deal and the family had to live in a trailer for a year). Describe the complication in a paragraph or two. Does this story have an influence on your life today?

How Escape Complicates Your Plots

1. Think of a time you have wanted to escape from a particular situation (a job, a relationship, your parents). Write a paragraph about how you escaped (physically or emotionally) or how you didn't escape. Did you make a plan? Did you act impulsively? Did you not act?

2. Think of a time you tried to escape from an overwhelming feeling—despair, anger, sadness, feeling emotionally smothered or restrained. Write a paragraph about what you did or didn't do to escape.

3. Think about a time that your need to escape complicated your love, mastery, or loss plot (you had to get out of that relationship, quit that job, escape the pain of caring for a dying friend). Write a paragraph describing how your escape attempt either resolved the conflict or made it worse.

How Sex Complicates Your Plots

1. Make two lists: your best and worst sexual experiences. Pick one of each, and write a paragraph describing how you felt and how you reacted. What decision about yourself and sex did you make because of these experiences? Which influenced your subsequent sexuality the most, the good experience or the bad one?
2. Make as many lists as you can: What turns you on sexually? What displeases you? What intrigues you? What frightens you? What do you like to give? What do you like to receive? What do you like to fantasize about but don't want to enact? Pick one item from each list and write a paragraph about it, describing either an experience that actually happened or a fantasy. Notice yourself as narrator. Does this describe how you are in life?
3. Think about the time that sex complicated your love, mastery, or loss plot (you slept with your best friend, you slept with your boss, you slept with someone you never saw again). Write a paragraph about the story of the conflict and its result. Did this result resolve the conflict? Did it deepen the complication until it dominated one of the plots? Tell how.

How Children Complicate Your Plots

If you have children, write a paragraph about how your life would be if you didn't have them. If you don't have children, write a paragraph about how your life would be if you did have them.

Think about how having children or not having children complicated your love, mastery, or loss plot (you got married to have children, having a child interferes with your dating life, you neglected your kids to further your career, you were afraid of losing a child and so never had one). Write a paragraph describing the situation. What was the conflict and its result? Did this result resolve the conflict? Did it deepen the complication until it dominated one of the plots? Tell how.

6

What Makes Sammy Run?
Reading Yourself and Others

I can read you like a book.
—Anonymous

The principal function of plot making is *interpretation:* how we make sense of what happens to us. You may believe that when you recount an experience you are simply describing, more or less objectively, an event and your reactions to it, without adding or subtracting any meaning, but this is almost never the case. In reality, you are always putting the event in whatever light seems to fit your plot.

Although we may have little or no control over some aspects of our lives, how we interpret them and what meaning we extract is up to us. To live an examined life means to scrutinize your plot, to learn how you write and enact your own story, and thus to unlock the mystery of why your life unfolds the way it does. We tell stories for many reasons: to instruct and to guide; to reveal or to battle; to create intimacy or distance; to express ourselves or to entertain; to seduce. We explain ourselves to others through stories. But the real function of the story is not to convey content but to reveal who we are. Similarly, the real function of plotting is to learn from it who we are and who others are. To be successful at plotting, we not only have to understand ourselves, we also have to be able to understand the characters of the people we come in contact with. So, while we write our own plots, we also "read" other people like a text. We do this by listening, observing, comparing, assessing. Is my new friend Max honest, intelligent, kind, and funny? Or behind his charming exterior does there lie the soul of a serial killer?

Making Sense of Events

A good interpretation will do one of two things: it will either resolve the questions you are turning over in your mind, providing a sense of peace and resolution of conflict; or it will do the opposite, agitating you further, magnetizing and drawing in related experiences, galvanizing you into searching through the past for data that support your new understanding. Even a good interpretation may be valid only for a limited time, giving way as you grow in maturity to a wiser or more rounded interpretation.

A good interpretation links together chunks of a person's behavior as understandable and revealing of their character. Some interpretations, of course, are more correct than others. For example, Roberta, desperate to save her marriage, decided to make some changes, and began by choosing the wrong interpretation:

When Stan said he thought we should separate, I was devastated. I knew it was my fault, and if I would just change some things about me he would stay. So I joined a health club, went on a diet, cut my hair, and started cooking gourmet meals every night. But he just seemed less interested than ever. In fact, he was annoyed by all the work I was doing on myself.

Roberta could interpret her situation in at least two ways: one, that she would never be good enough for her husband because she was too far gone to ever be lovable; or two, that her husband had already made up his mind to leave her and nothing she did would affect his decision.

We use plot making not only to arrange experiences into a story and thereby impose an interpretation on them but also to screen out certain categories of experience. If you believe yourself to be uneducated and unintelligent, for example, you will probably avoid people and situations that you fear will expose your vulnerability, such as discussing a novel or film with friends who take such things seriously.

More insidiously, plot can screen out self-knowledge. This defensive function of plot is very powerful and easily overlooked. It is just as important to scrutinize what our plots protect us from as what they permit us to have.

Harry was an agoraphobic who experienced panic attacks if he ventured too far from home. Whenever an invitation or appointment required traveling outside the narrow orbit of places he defined as safe, he convinced himself that he was too tired or ill, or that the movie being shown wasn't very good, or that the company was boring, or that he ought to stay home and work. He viewed each declined outing as one of a kind, never recognizing the pattern of fear and avoidance. Not until he examined his behavior in therapy did he realize that his plot of illness, overwork, and unsociability had been shielding him from both the terrifying emotions of helplessness in "unsafe" places and the deeper implications of his systematic refusals to go out.

Defenses hide the plot of the real self—the vulnerable self, your authentic self. When you get stuck in your plotting— when you find yourself spinning your wheels in life—it's probably because you are writing from your defensive plot rather than your authentic one.

The correct interpretation is the one that exposes your feelings rather than your strategies to hide your feelings. For example, after a brilliant graduate thesis, Alice seemed headed toward an equally brilliant career as a historian. At the same time, she completely neglected her appearance, and seemed to have almost no awareness of herself as a physical presence. When she became aware that her appearance might hold her back from making progress in her academic career, she decided to address it in therapy.

> When I was a child, my mother would always brag to her friends about my awards; but she would always criticize my choice of clothing or the way I combed my hair. It was painful, because I really did care how I looked. But I never got one compliment from her. After a while I learned to just tune out her criticisms and only hear the praise. I guess I stopped thinking about my appearance—if I was invisible in this way, then it wouldn't matter, would it?

Most people have acquired this kind of emotional misinformation that prevents them from seeing themselves as they really are. Once internalized, these hypercritical judgments— "I'm ugly," "I'm dumb"—make you chronically fearful or sad. To avoid painful exposure of your feelings, you develop ways to defend and hide your vulnerability. You show an armored self to the world. Over time, you may lose touch with what you are defending and mistake the defensive self for the real one. Since the genesis of your distress is not addressed, it is not open to revision.

Until you face your fears, desires, and angers, you cannot write an authentic plot based on your true strengths and weaknesses. Just as a doctor can't examine your body unless you take your clothes off, you cannot get an accurate reading of what is emotionally true for you until your defensive strategies have been put aside and your "unacceptable" emotions examined.

If the defensive strategy runs long enough, it may take some effort to remember what it was you were originally trying to protect. For example, "It isn't that I wanted to have sex with everyone I went out with, it's just that I couldn't think of anything to talk to them about—I was shy and inarticulate."

Luanna's defensive story was that she had a good life and just didn't want to have children. But her authentic story turned out to be something quite different. Luanna, a forty-year-old architect, was very devoted to her career, her husband, and their two dalmatians. She had always known that she didn't want to have children. When she came into treatment after her mother died, she spent a good deal of time exploring that relationship. Although she initially described it as "good, normal—like everyone else's," it soon became clear that Luanna was terrified of turning out like her mother, whom she saw as a miserable woman who had been greatly disappointed by life. Her mother had taken out her misery on Luanna, criticizing and punishing her for every infraction. Upon reflection, Luanna realized that her authentic plot was, "I don't want to have children because I'm afraid I'll be as cruel to them as my mother was to me."

Defensive strategies can become plot elements in and of themselves. You may be so successful at acting hard and aggressive to hide your vulnerability, for example, that people believe you are tough and treat you accordingly. Or you may spend your life making money because you feel poor and precarious, yet as you become more financially secure, your anxieties are intensified rather than assuaged; ten times as much money means ten times as many worries.

Pitfalls of Interpretation

An event becomes experience only in the telling, and this telling inevitably recasts the event in two important ways: by confusing interpretations with facts, and by summarizing and selecting.

We frequently confuse interpretations or conclusions with facts. Have you ever called the doctor and said, "I have a sinus infection," only to have the doctor ask you a series of questions about what your actual symptoms are? The doctor wants facts, not the conclusion you have drawn, even if your conclusion is correct. Or your teenage daughter returns home very late from a date, and you shout at her. When she calls her friends later, she complains that you were "abusive." This is her interpretation, based on the fact that you were anxious and upset enough to raise your voice in anger. Your interpretation, of course, would probably be quite different.

We also recast events by *summarizing* and *selecting*— choosing salient details and leaving out others—to slant the account toward an interpretation, making a case for ourselves as a certain kind of person. This is true even if, as is often the case, we do not tell most of our stories to anyone. We still mentally replay the event, trying on various interpretations and descriptions. Most of us do this several times a day without realizing it.

For example, Gail met an interesting man at a party. They seemed to hit it off, and exchanged phone numbers. That night, after she got home, she was very excited and felt that a new romance was definitely in the offing. By the next evening, when he hadn't called, she reinterpreted the same events and decided that he had just given her his phone number to be polite. She went into a tailspin and felt very sorry for herself for a whole day. Finally, she told herself that she was just being paranoid and should call him to see how he really felt.

As we grow in understanding and self-knowledge, it becomes easier and even exciting to revise our interpretations of events. Let's look at a couple of concepts that will help you to break unconstructive patterns of interpretation and adopt new ones.

Connect the Dots

Interpreting the events in our lives to fit our plot is a lot like the child's game of connect the dots: the events in your life are fixed, like the dots, but you can redraw the connections between them to form different pictures. As your understanding of yourself and others deepens, you may think back to a situation and realize that another interpretation fits the facts better than the one you have accepted for years. For instance, you remember your parents' anger when you came into their bedroom for just one more goodnight kiss, hours after they had put you to bed. In retrospect, you now see that they were probably irritated at being interrupted when they wanted to make love, rather than because they wanted to make sure you got plenty of sleep.

Interpretation doesn't allow us to alter the sequence of events, but it does give us the freedom to decide which events to include in a particular plot and how much space and weight to give them. Clearly, the house cannot be on fire before you strike the match, childhood cannot occur after your college graduation, nor can you fall in love with a handsome stranger whom you have known for several years. As in a game of connect the dots, the final picture depends on how you number the dots, and errors here can skew your interpretation. For example, you may think that your friend didn't invite you to her party because of the critical things you said about her lover, but it is also possible that she sent out the invitations before that fateful conversation. Or your coworker comes in and stalks past you without saying hello. First you assume she's mad at you because you told the boss she left an hour early on Friday. But she may have a backache from sleeping on the couch after a fight with her boyfriend, or have lost a winning lottery ticket, or be worried about her AIDS test results.

Be Flexible

It's important to be flexible when you interpret events. The more complexity and nuance you can comfortably accept, the freer you are to envision new stories for yourself to enact. For example, Peter could never imagine standing up to his wife when she was upset with him. Her crying seemed to silence his point of view. Since his own parents had fought a great deal, and the fights always ended with his mother in tears, a man who made a woman cry seemed to him to be a monster. His wife was aware of her power over him and used tears to bring about Peter's submission. One day, while telling his friend this story, Peter realized that his wife was really bullying him with her tears—just as his father bullied his mother with his abusive ravings. With this new interpretation of his wife's reaction, he was able to argue effectively with her and not back down.

Flexibility arises from the realization that no single cause accounts for an action or event. This is particularly true where other people are concerned. In fact, although you may succeed in deepening your understanding, some events may elude your search for a complete explanation. Is it because you lost weight that Judy wants to sleep with you after shunning you for months? Or because her boyfriend left her? Or both, or neither? Perhaps she read a novel or heard a piece of music that prompted an obscure movement in her soul, causing her to see you in a new light. How can you know, when she herself may be unable to tell you?

Making Sense of Episodes

Episodes are events or circumstances that just drop into our lives and seem to have no connection with our ongoing plot. Often, they have no meaning other than to serve as catalysts that bring us from one stage of our plot into another. One of the pitfalls of interpretation is to try to attribute too much meaning to episodes. Not every romance can be the love of your life; not every friendship can be lifelong; not every job can be a career or a vocation; and not every blunder (fortunately) is permanent. Often, things just come naturally to an end when you've gotten what you could out of them—or they out of you.

For example, Brooke, a magazine editor, was happy in her relationship with Alan. They had been dating for months, and were talking about moving in together. One day at work she met Theresa, a writer who was in town from another state to talk about a story. They both felt an instant connection. They had a flirtatious conversation, made a date, and spent the next three nights making passionate love at Theresa's hotel. Then Theresa flew back home, her business in the city over.

Brooke was really shaken up. She had never felt attracted to a woman before, and having spontaneous sex with anyone, man or woman, was totally out of character for her. She just never did things like that. And now, after three days of intensity, it was over, as if it had never existed. What was she supposed to make of that? Did it mean she was really gay? Did it mean she wasn't in love with Alan? Did it mean she was lying and deceitful? Brooke drove herself crazy trying to figure out the deeper meaning of this episode.

Finally, she decided that the episode was just that: a spontaneous moment of joy in her life. On reflection, she realized that she actually felt revitalized by it, and was surprised to discover that she really wanted to make a commitment to Alan. She suggested that instead of living together, they make plans to get married.

Just as we don't know beforehand what sort of characters we're dealing with in a situation or relationship, we can't tell what its meaning and duration might be, either. Episodes are like digressions in your life's narrative. They may form part of the plot later, when you have achieved a point of view that permits you to see that larger pattern. Or they remain like islands in your experience—incidents that have a completeness of their own without ever becoming closely related or well integrated into the main themes of your life.

Some episodes, like Brooke's, are catalysts—short bursts whose purpose is to move you along the path of your development. Other episodes are more lengthy. They may seem like time killers, but they may really be stepping stones. For example, Amy had always been very imaginative as a child, and longed to be a writer or an actress. Her parents, who were first-generation Chinese Americans, wanted her to go to law school, and she found herself working in a law firm that practiced injury law. Her reports were always laced with detail and interesting language, which her superiors found a waste of time. She had two negative reviews from her boss and was put on probation. When she thought about why she was failing at this firm, she realized that she simply didn't belong there; she belonged in litigation, where she could put her language and dramatic skills to productive use. She applied for a job in the D.A.'s office and has been happily working there ever since. When she recalls her time in injury law, she sees it as an episode, a place where she was able to learn what she was truly suited for in life.

It is useful to identify episodes as such and not stretch their significance. Often, however, it is difficult to identify an episode as such as it is occurring. In fact, sometimes you can only tell in retrospect. A rule of thumb is that episodes are time fillers, not meaningful and unplottable, whereas subplots become meaningfully linked to other events. A life of episodes equals a life of noncommitment.

Some events, however, will only be episodes, and finding

that acceptable is part of the process of recognition. Unfortunately, we may view episodes not merely as endings but as failures. This is almost always a false reading. Not every relationship or situation improves with age. For example, when Brooke thought about Theresa, she realized that they had very little in common and that three days was probably as much intimacy as they could sustain. If their affair had not of necessity been sandwiched into a business trip, it might have dragged on with recriminations and pain.

Think back on a few such episodes in your own life that ended. Even if you were not the one who ended them, can you honestly say you're not glad at least some of them are over? Furthermore, finding endings painful does not mean that you truly needed or loved what you lost, or that it was in your best interest. It may simply mean that you have trouble with endings, as many of us do. We get ourselves into situations from which we have a hard time extricating ourselves, yet we recognize the necessity of ending them. As Bob Dylan sang about this 20/20 hindsight, "I hate myself for loving you and I'm glad the curtain fell."

When a situation levels out, is it a failure? Not necessarily. Constantly evolving isn't always better; more of what's good may be a diminishment, not an enhancement. For example, your marriage may be wonderful with one child, and a disaster with two.

Difficulties with episodes can occur because you want to make a serious commitment, yet this isn't the right time, place, or set of characters for it. We often waste effort on such dead-end situations. When something seems to end for no reason, it's good to remember that certain situations (like vacations) just have short lifespans.

Remember too that episodes are not the same as failures. Not everything is meant to last, but that does not diminish its value and may even deepen its beauty. When you think about it, the idea of a relationship as an "investment" of emotion is a rather materialistic and stingy way of looking at things. It implies that you have only so much love, and that if you spend it on a person who doesn't return it, this irreplaceable love has been lost or squandered and the lover defrauded. I am not arguing for lack of responsibility in our emotional connections with others, but rather the opposite; some relationships are worth working on and others are not. Of course, knowing how to tell the difference is not easy and is based on how well you can read other people's character.

Problems of Scale

Problems of scale—blowing things out of proportion, making light of things that are really important—can get in the way of a good interpretation. We often make mistakes of scale in the early stages of an episode, when it most resembles a main plot.

For example, perhaps you have been very lonely since you broke up with your girlfriend a year ago. You begin an affair with a woman of whom you're very fond, although you know that ultimately there is no potential for a long-term relationship. But you soon find yourself behaving just as you did when you were really in love. You are more vulnerable to this woman than is appropriate, even though you know at a deep level that you're not really well matched. You have made a mistake of scale: your feelings for this woman loomed larger than they should have because there was nothing else on your emotional horizon to compare them with. When you have no reference point, crossing paths with the garbage man each week can start to seem like a fateful encounter.

It's also easy to make the opposite mistake, failing to see the true importance of some element in your life. Let's say you have a great apartment with a view that makes your city look like a fishing village on the Mediterranean. It is spacious, light, and beautifully proportioned. Then you lose the apartment and move elsewhere. Life seems suddenly dark, shabby, cramped, and ungracious. You have undervalued something central to your plot—in this case, a setting—because it was so familiar that you ranked it too low on the scale of importance. You didn't realize that your view of life was really the view from your beautiful apartment.

Supporting Characters: Reading Your Roles with Others

Who Are These People and Why Are They in My Story?

Everyone who figures in the events of your life can be incorporated into your story as a major or minor character. As you begin to pay attention to the stories you tell, you may see that similar characters recur frequently in your life—"Why do I always pick guys who dump me?" "Every woman I meet is like my mother." These insights can give you the power to create new, more multidimensional characters. You should remember that you are also playing roles in other people's stories, roles that may be very different from the one you have created for yourself.

Much of the storytelling people do for others has seduction as its subtext. By seduction I do not necessarily mean sexual seduction, although that may be involved. People shape each story to please their listeners, to win them over to their plight, cause, personality, or point of view. They want their listeners to share their concerns, to be beguiled by the self they have presented. In this sense, people are pedestrian Scheherazades, seeking favor by continuously entertaining and seducing with tales. This form of storytelling rests on a willed, expressive *presentation* of the self, and the emphasis is on the content of the story. Among the stories people tell about themselves, this is the authorized biography.

People always seek to portray themselves in a positive way. Don't lose track of the hidden instruction in each story: "Accept me. Believe me. Like me." Unfortunately, no one ever adds, "I am a total liar—don't believe a word I say!" or, "The last four people who got involved with me thought it was the worst experience of their lives. Throw me out of your house now!"

When we listen to a story, we have to observe the storyteller and assess the match between what we know of the teller and how he depicts himself. This form of storytelling has to do with *exposure* of the self—of the internal story maker and plotter—and the emphasis is on the process rather than the anecdotal content of the story. For example, if Katherine tells you that she almost never drinks alcohol, yet whenever you see her she's making an exception because of a terrible day at work or the receipt of good news, you can safely draw some conclusions not only about her drinking, but also about her level of honesty and personal insight.

What you have witnessed is a strategy of lying to oneself by making frequent exceptions to self-imposed rules. In this example, the anecdote presented by the teller ("You wouldn't believe what an awful day I had at work today") contradicts the process inadvertently exposed by the teller ("Every day I find a reason to drink, but I act as if these reasons are not connected"). Remember, the stories people tell themselves are not the same as the stories they tell others, and their version of the events in their lives is not the same as the spin that others consistently observe them putting on things.

People reveal themselves in small, unrelated fragments, and to understand them we have to step back so that the distance permits us to discern larger patterns and shapes. After you listen to someone's stories for a while, you will begin to notice themes: "You can't trust anyone, everyone's out to screw you." "The world is going to hell in a handbasket! This would never have happened in the good old days." "I am brilliant but unappreciated at what I do, and anyone would be lucky to have my approval." From these themes, and from the details of a person's behavior, a cohesive picture begins to emerge that almost invariably differs from the one your acquaintance would recognize in the mirror.

Pay Attention to the Fate of Other Characters

Pay attention to what happened to the other characters in the stories people tell you, particularly your new acquaintances. If they are still around and happily functioning in the person's life, perhaps in a changed role, this is a good sign. But if they're wearing a (metaphorical) cement suit, watch out. Be aware that you may well share the fate of the previous characters in your new friend's stories. If your date's ex-girlfriends aren't speaking to him, chances are you won't be, either. It is the height of self-deception to believe that you alone will be treated differently, or will be able to break the spell and change the pattern. Movies and song lyrics support this heroic notion, but life itself does not. The power of love alone cannot cure anyone of compulsive womanizing, gambling, or substance abuse.

Real engagement with a person is impossible unless you believe the person's story and see situations from the person's point of view. When you meet someone you like and listen to the stories of his or her interaction with others, you identify with *that person*. When you become disenchanted, however, you begin to identify more with the stories of people who have complained about that person, and you come to see what others have found difficult about this person:

> When I first met Bill, he told me that he really wanted to be in an intimate relationship, but that most of the women he seemed to meet were too critical—he just couldn't seem to get close to them. I sympathized because I know a lot of critical

women. My sympathy lasted until our second date, when he was two hours late and didn't even call. When I called him on it, he said, "Women are always so picky and hostile to me." That was it for me—I guess I joined a long line of critical ex-girlfriends.

This point of view is poison for a potential relationship. And it also applies to you. Let's say you are complaining about your ex-wife to your date, a divorcee; if she seems unsympathetic or worse, you might consider that her point of view as listener to this story is much closer to your ex-wife's than to yours. It's less natural for her to be empathic toward your position.

Words and Actions

If you perceive a conflict between someone's words and actions, you should *always* go by the behavior. The bottom line is action, not language. A mismatch between text and action often indicates that an unknown subplot is being acted out. What the story says contains a germ of this subplot.

I was dating this guy, Larry, and he looked right in my eyes and told me, "When I'm truly in love with someone, like I am with you, it's impossible for me to be attracted to another woman." I have to admit, I was flattered beyond belief. But the next week we went out to dinner, and every time an attractive woman walked by our table, he would stare at her—he'd even lose track of our conversation!

In this example, the subplot is the disavowal of sexual attraction. Put a mental bookmark on that subplot and see if it develops into something larger.

Are You a Plot or a Subplot?

Just as some people are more important than others in your life, when someone becomes important to you, you need to ascertain whether the person regards you as part of a major plot or a subplot. Martin, recently divorced, had been having an affair with Ava. Every time Ava wept in Martin's arms, complaining that her husband paid her no attention or criticized her, Martin hoped she would end her marriage. While this outcome was a decided possibility, it was equally likely that she would stay in her marriage forever.

When you do manage to coerce someone into the behavior you prefer—when he or she agrees, reluctantly, for example, not to sleep with other people—the issue will inevitably come up again as a subplot. Your victory is a hollow one. Incident springs out of character, and you can't negotiate character. Likewise, when someone you know does something totally unexpected, like having an affair or quitting her job, this action has its source in a subplot that was running simultaneously. Either you didn't hear that parallel story, or you misread the other person. If you look back over your interactions with that person, however, you will always find clues about the subplot you chose to ignore or misinterpreted.

Rereading Others

When more of a person's character is revealed and it doesn't fit with, or even obliterates, what you think is true about that person, how do you reconcile this new information with your existing read on his character? First, remember that character has to be revealed over time in increments, depicted by deed and action, not talk and self-description. Pay more attention to how people treat you and others, and less attention to how they say they're treating you. As E. M. Forster said, "A chance word or a sigh are just as much evidence as a speech or a murder: the life they reveal ceases to be secret and enters the realm of action."

Second, remember that when you are invested in the wrong read about another person, loss is inevitable. If you are convinced that your child is destined to be a doctor, but he grows up to be a stained glass artist, you will have to mourn the loss of your "doctor child" before you can begin to understand your real child. If you believe that your employees love working for your "corporate family," and then find out that they are considering striking for higher wages, you will have to mourn the loss of your old image of them before you can contend with their real needs.

Third, knowing people involves testing your hypotheses about them. This means that you must talk to them. Ask questions. If you think your married lover might not really want to leave his wife, despite his proclamations of undying love for you, ask. If he responds that he does indeed want to leave his wife, ask, "When?" This involves some risk taking, which is why we are often more willing to believe words than actions when we think we may be hurt by the truth. But as we have said, if you are invested in the wrong read, you're going to experience loss anyway. At least this way you're in control, you can have the satisfaction of confirming your intuitive feelings, and you can sharpen your character-reading skills so you don't make the same mistake in the future.

Finally, don't forget that in our readings of others, all meanings and conclusions are tentative. We read others over and over. Even decisions that endure are usually redecided on more subtle levels. Commitments, by their nature, must be frequently reaffirmed as we react to destabilizing forces or events. Just as writing your plot is a continuous activity, so is reading other people, for they are always changing, however minutely.

Wishful Seeing: Pitfalls of Reading Others

We are not innocent or objective readers of others' plots because we look for what we want to see. We project our assumptions and needs onto others, and convert emotional cues into personality descriptions. For example, you meet a woman who tells you how deeply she loved her old boyfriend. You read her as someone who is capable of profound emotional connection and think, "She'd be a great girlfriend—she's open and loyal." But it may be that she is only capable of loving what she's *lost*.

It is this tendency to translate our requirements into "facts" about others at which Jane Austen gently poked fun in the first sentence of *Pride and Prejudice:* "It is a truth universally acknowledged, that a single man in possession of a fortune, must be in want of a wife." The more likely a person is to conveniently fit our needs and dreams, the less likely we are to see him or her clearly.

Splitting

One source of trouble in reading others is called *splitting,* a psychological defense mechanism that consists of keeping in separate compartments feelings about others that are either all positive or all negative. You may suddenly and completely shift back and forth from the extreme positive to the extreme negative internal image of a particular person—you're a goddess/ you're a whore—without being able to achieve a stable image strong enough to contain the conflicting feelings. Splitting can occur in two ways. You can split your external world into two camps—for example, WASPs are good, Jews are bad. Or you can split your feelings for one person or thing down the middle—for example, your wonderful wife and your dreadful wife. Usually when people fall from grace, it's a long way down.

Splitting has to do with how you contain and where you place your negative feelings about people to whom you are attached. For example, when Rick broke up with Helen, he saw her as all bad, while his new girlfriend, Maude, could do no wrong; this protected him from the love and vulnerability he still felt toward Helen, while also protecting him from the realization that Maude had some less-than-wonderful qualities.

You can feel split within yourself between conflicting feelings of love and hate that you feel for the same person. For example, Donna's husband, Todd, frequently stayed out late drinking with the boys, but he always brought her a thoughtful present to make amends. She almost simultaneously experienced pleasure at receiving the gift, which was always accompanied by a loving embrace and sincere apology, and frustration that no matter how many times she asked him to stay home with her, he invariably went out with his friends. Inside, she held in close proximity images of the loving Todd and the insensitive Todd.

Eventually, she became extremely ambivalent in her feelings toward her husband; she wasn't able to integrate her two incompatible attitudes about him. As a consequence, she never saw Todd as a whole person. She either thought he was a great guy—idealizing him as unrealistically good and powerful—or she experienced outbursts of fury in which she called him all the vile names she could think of. Remember, the only way off the pedestal is down!

The way to integrate the positive and negative qualities you perceive in a person or a group is to keep your eyes open and simply observe, without ardor or enmity, and without taking the behavior personally. The better you know someone, the harder it is either to idealize or despise that person. Look for resemblances rather than differences between you and others. The growing sense of solidarity and kinship you experience permits you to accept people's good and bad qualities with greater equanimity—after all, they are not really so different from you.

Once you see others more clearly, it will be easier to take responsibility for the choices you've made, which may mean accepting the loss of a fantasy. You may have dreamed of being a father, yet the love of your life is a woman who doesn't want children. Can you come to terms with the loss of your dream without blaming your wife? Eliminating idealization and vilification means resolving the loss of a desire.

When you, as narrator of your story, split off bad qualities from good qualities, or bad people from good, it limits your plot possibilities and creates flat, unrealistic characters and predictable sequences of events. Saints and villains are not capable, as characters, of much development, and their actions are circumscribed as a result. It is impossible to have honest, subtle, durable relationships with people whom you've portrayed as utterly good or bad. When characters in your plot look this way to you, it's time to reappraise them and try to read them more accurately.

Projection

Projection—attributing to others your own wishes, feelings, and motivations—also contributes to faulty plot making. For example, Ann wrote a book and was interviewed about it on the radio. When she got home, she was very upset that her best friend, Rebecca, had not called to congratulate her, even though Rebecca had told her she was going to listen. If Rebecca had been interviewed, Ann would have phoned her immediately with excitement and praise, and this was the way she expected her friend to behave toward her. Ann did not consider, however, that Rebecca, by not making a fuss, was treating her how *she* likes to be treated.

Ann was trying to make Rebecca fit into her notion of how Rebecca should feel and be. But such a preconceived way of finishing a plot never works, because it doesn't take other people's reality into consideration. The characteristics that you project onto others are usually true about you, not them, and so you are forever interacting with yourself.

Projection reveals disavowed parts of the speaker's character. If you are scrupulously honest and someone accuses you of lying, for example, you can be certain that the person finds lying easy or justifiable. The man who assumes that all the attractive women he meets are dying to have a relationship with him, and that they will come running if he winks his eye, reveals only his own narcissism, promiscuity, and inability to sustain interest in others as human beings.

Just as the color and action of a movie obscures the reality of the blank white screen behind it, projection closes our eyes to the full meaning of what is before us. For example, you might assume that if Jeannie calls you night after night to have dinner, she really cares about you, but the truth is that she just doesn't like eating alone and you are her only available friend.

One way that we project is to extend small bits of others' behavior into character descriptions. For example, while Antonio and Daphne were engaged, he was extremely neat and vacuumed his apartment frequently. After they were married, however, he never touched the vacuum again. Vacuuming was okay for him when he was single, but once he married it became unthinkable—housekeeping was a woman's responsibility. Daphne, however, had taken his behavior as evidence that neatness was part of his character. After all, that's what her own vacuuming meant about her!

Our projections speak volumes, but only about ourselves. Here's Greta's story:

> I fell madly in love with a married man, Henry, and—to his surprise—he fell madly in love with me. We had an intense, year-long affair. This was definitely not an infatuation. It seemed to me that it was time for Henry to make the break from his wife—I knew for a fact that he spent more time with me than he did with her. Unbelievably, he told me that he had decided to stay in his marriage, which he admitted was a part-

nership without passion, "for the sake of the children."

I was devastated. I just couldn't understand how he could do this. For me, passion and intimacy are everything. It took me another year without him to realize that these were my priorities, not Henry's. For him, tranquillity and familiarity were safer and therefore preferable.

We project good intentions and feelings onto others just as frequently as we do the bad. For example, we may not recognize disloyal or duplicitous behavior in others because we find ourselves incapable of it; if we are honest, we may be the last to notice the evidence that someone has cheated us.

Stereotypes are a global form of projection, and they tend to be negative. When you give authority to stereotypes in your readings of other people—poor people are lazy, beautiful women are dumb, all men are manipulative—you write a fraudulent plot in advance. People who think in stereotypes project onto others certain kinds of plot possibilities and limitations. Stereotypes are always about a failure of the imagination in terms of plot making. They are linked to the egotism of the child's point of view because they result from an insufficient sense of the reality of others as individuals.

Expectations

Remedying projection in our plot making requires taking a hard look at our expectations of others. Most of us are very attached to our expectations, yet it is crucial to find some way of testing them. There is pain connected with examining and consequently losing cherished expectations. However, loss—especially loss of illusions—adds beauty and depth to your plot.

It is important to embrace your experiences, even if they're painful, because they give you a past and make you feel that you have *lived* your life. The sadness you experience is *your* sadness. Your experiences, your plot, your life, is all that you have. Love affairs may hurt, for example, but they also make you feel that you have lived, have participated fully in your life. The capacity for joy in life is intimately connected with the capacity for risk taking. The experience of loss adds richness to your plot. Wisdom resides in affirming your past, since life is an ongoing process.

We cannot exist without expectations—if we didn't expect to wake up in the morning and live another day, we couldn't get much done—yet our expectations are often erroneous. Expectations complete the story, but they can be based on the wrong premise. For example, maybe you want to rescue your lover, whom you believe to be in distress, because if you were in the same situation you would want to be rescued. However, you need to consider the possibility that she doesn't want to be rescued and may even resent you for trying. She may prefer the familiarity of that "distress," or she may want to find the solution herself.

In general, given the information at one's disposal, many interpretations probably fit. Openness about the data and flexibility about cause and effect are the keys to good interpretations. Be gentle with yourself—you can't be right all the time. It's more realistic to approach expectations like a batting average: .400 is terrific, but that means you have hit the ball less than half the time!

Whether you see the cup as half full or half empty has to do with your expectations and your interpretations of others' behavior—what you think the experience defines about the emotional transactions in which you participate. Being in a marriage where you make love once a week may make you feel unsatisfied and deprived, as if there are only a few drops at the bottom of the cup, but your husband may feel that this is a lot of sexuality for a long-term relationship, so for him the cup is running over. How flexible are you in assigning meaning, and how able are you to imagine other possible interpretations? As in the film *Rashomon,* many different viewpoints on and constructions of a situation can be valid.

As we discussed earlier, plotting your life is like a game of "connect the dots"—the dots are the events of your life and you connect them into patterns representing your plot. Our expectations create a selective focus, determining which experiences we designate as trivial or irrelevant and which we consider important enough to choose as a "dot," or significant event. You decide which dots to include, which affects the possible configurations you can create by connecting them.

Overreading and Underreading

Determining what conclusions we may legitimately draw from the behavior of others and the stories they tell us is a fascinating and difficult enterprise. Reading too much in—attaching too much significance to nuances of behavior—can be as disastrous as not reading in enough. Although much can be guessed at quickly, little can be decided because it takes time to glean enough fragments to be able to step back and see the pattern emerge, to identify which elements are indicative of character and which of caprice.

Our assumptions and expectations complete the story, yet they can easily be based on the wrong premise. For example, when Jane confronted her boss on his attitude toward the people he supervised, her colleague Frank thought that she must be very fearless to speak up to him in such a direct way. But when Frank complimented her on this later, she told him it wasn't fearlessness at all. She just didn't care if she got fired because her husband had recently gotten a big raise at his job. Similarly, Bill had a rude awakening when he found out that his assumptions about a new group of friends were diametrically opposed to the truth:

> My wife and I got into this new social group, some really nice couples. These people respected each other, they were nice to

one another, they shared child care and household chores—
they were great. In fact, I was chagrined because my wife and
I don't get along as well as these couples seemed to. So I was
blown completely out of the water when I discovered that the
husband of couple A and the wife of couple B had been having
an affair for two years, while the wife of couple A and the husband of couple C had recently become an item. I really had to
question my perception of reality. When I thought back, I realized that I had completely misinterpreted some clues based
on my own assumptions that they were happily married.

When we look back with the benefit of hindsight, we often
discover that our early impressions were indeed borne out by
experience. Yet interpretation doesn't really work unless you
have a broad base with many possibilities from which to spec-
ulate about what a person's behavior may mean about their
character.

When you first meet someone, you can't tell if he or she
will turn out to be a major character, a walk-on, or a cameo
appearance by someone who's important for another reason.
It is nearly impossible to tell what roles people will play in
your life. We may berate ourselves later for wasting time and
energy with someone who turned out to play only a minor
role, but this is unfair—it was an episode and as such served
its purpose. We need to distinguish between what we can and
cannot know at the beginning of a relationship. It is equally
difficult to tell whether someone will be enormously important to us. The plot of "love at first sight"—of instant recognition—happens less often than is popularly supposed. It is a
plot that works powerfully upon the imagination, however,
and it has hindsight in its favor.

All the World's a Stage

In the early stages of a relationship, you are reading, listening, scanning, and speculating a great deal in order to learn as much of the other person's story as quickly as possible, and because the stakes are high you have a lot of anxiety. Further, it is almost impossible to know at what point in someone else's plot you have entered his or her life. This is the problem of timing, and it refers to whether your plot and the other's have reached compatible points. The man who looked like a frog at one point in your life may look like a prince later. You might have wonderful chemistry with someone who regretfully acknowledges that the timing is wrong—he has not yet recovered from the painful effects of a recent divorce.

Throughout our lives we play many roles in others' plots, perhaps even simultaneously playing very different roles. As a woman, for example, you may be ambivalent about the idea of having children and still be a good mother, or be both a betrayed wife in your marriage and a desired mistress to your lover. Sometimes it's not clear which role you're playing. You may believe you're playing the home-wrecker by having an affair with a married woman, while in truth she is both more satisfied sexually and more guilt stricken, so she goes out of her way to be attentive to her husband and value his good qualities. Unwittingly, your role is to provide the "glue" that keeps their marriage together.

The Audition

You may unwittingly be auditioning for a part in someone else's plot. This sounds facetious, but it does describe a certain kind of encounter. For example, at age thirty-five, Dan decided that now was the correct time to marry and have children, so he superimposed his imagined image of his future wife over each woman that he dated, checking for a good fit. He was looking for someone with a particular background, set of options, and pedigree, and when he found the right one, he married her.

People like Dan, who search for people with certain options, often defer searching for character, and those who conduct auditions are not looking for surprises—although they often get them. A few years later, Dan says:

> I was ready to get married and have kids. When I met Pam I thought she was perfect: she was beautiful, intelligent, successful, interested in children, and she was a Methodist, like me. I thought she was the most steady, calm woman I had ever met. We fell in love and got married. I thought I'd really made a smart move. But after the first year, it became clear that she was actually the opposite of what I had thought she was—she wasn't calm, she was rigid, and she had a whole raft of personal problems that she refused to acknowledge. We had a lot of issues to resolve.

Trophies and Props

You may also be cast in the part of prop or trophy. If you are a prop or a trophy in someone else's plot, you assist that person's ends, even if unwittingly. You function primarily for something in that person's plot, not the other way around; your usefulness to the person defines you.

A prop role can be summed up satisfactorily in one phrase: to have a role in someone else's life. For example, Cynthia was adopted because her adoptive mother decided that the family needed a second child to keep the first child company. She never really thought of Cynthia as a person with needs to be addressed and a character to be nurtured, but as someone to complete photographs and fill up the house and be a companion for the first child. Some people treat their attractive dates as fashion accessories who are pleasant to sleep with and dine out with. In the plot of a narcissist, all others are props, since true attachment is antithetical to narcissism.

Trophies are defined by the degree to which possessing them adds luster to one's reputation, because of either the trophy's looks, money, or fame. For example, the successful businessman who, now that his children are grown, divorces the wife who put him through school and marries a gorgeous twenty-three-year-old is so common as to be a cliché. However, while a prop is at least a supporting character in someone else's drama, a trophy has no personhood at all; in fact, when the trophy's human needs become apparent, they are greeted with resentment.

Although you may prefer not to think about it, it is entirely possible that you have cast some people as trophies or props in your own life (for example, the roommate who functioned as nothing but a rent payer; the airhead you dated in college because you enjoyed the looks you got when the two of you were together). Now think about your own place in those people's lives. Do you function at a similar level of unimportance for them? If there is a wide disparity between the reciprocal roles—for example, if you are merely a prop in someone's drama while that person is a fully dimensional character in yours—you need to examine whether the situation really fits your needs.

Bit Players

You may also play a bit role in someone's plot. A bit player is more than a prop but less than a fully dimensional character. Here, your importance to the plot is limited by your function as teacher, neighbor, mentor, and so forth. Outside the confines of the role, or after it ends, the relationship may not survive.

Role Playing

We play multiple roles, in both our own plots and those of others, often at the same time. In the last chapter of your plot, you may have been the sexually unfulfilled wife; in this chapter, with someone else, you play the role of sex goddess. You can be the client in your lawyer's office and the lawyer in your own office. The same person can be the good wife, the sensual mistress, the baby hater, the dutiful mother, and the capable doctor. Our identity, in terms of the roles we play in each plot, is fluid. This fact should be a source of wonder and empathy, as well as lending elasticity and suppleness to your plot.

We play different roles depending on whom we consort with, but your plot goes on beyond the person you're with. Certainly, important relationships tend to blur the edges of who you are, but people sometimes think their relationships actually define them. For example, being a mother or wife can overshadow a woman's experience of herself as a separate person so strongly that when her children grow up or her husband leaves her, she doesn't know who she is. Working men and women often feel defined by their jobs in this way, and undergo a crushing sense of loss when they lose their positions.

As we saw earlier, people reveal their embeddedness in roles by simple linguistic choices. For example, when your friend Brent refers to his wife (whom you know very well) as "my wife" rather than "Mary," his choice of words is descriptive of his embedded role. He isn't talking to you, but to himself. When Brent says, "My wife" (rather than "Mary") "is putting on her jewelry," he is in a reverie about her as his wife and himself as her husband; he is not speaking about Mary as a person. This is also true when someone says "my child/daughter/son" to someone who knows the child well.

It's possible to get stuck in a role and think that role defines you. "I'm a boss, not a secretary." "I'm a rich person, not a poor person." "I'm married, not single." This attitude creates an us-versus-them dynamic. People see the Other as frightening and terrible, even though (or perhaps because) they have been that Other themselves. When your life changes and you advance in terms of your power in the world, one of the things you gain is the chance to play a new role. Often we have such shame about having been powerless, or less powerful, that we seek to distance ourselves from the former role. We disavow the powerlessness and the previous self that went with it. Being without power is frightening, so we tell ourselves a story that it didn't happen and try to make that story true.

But in truth your power, or lack of it, doesn't define you as a self—it merely opens or closes up plot possibilities. We get embedded in our roles and forget that our experiences make it possible to empathize with others.

Story making is not about making up what didn't happen or disavowing what did. It is about encompassing the richness of what *did* happen. The way to do this is to acknowledge the inherent multiplicity of roles in our lives, and not become embedded in any single one. The more roles you can remember and acknowledge playing, the greater your empathy or solidarity with others.

When you meet someone new, you may offer that person a part in your ongoing drama or you may be offered a part in that person's drama. But it's also possible to create a new plot together, one based on desire rather than need. Creating a plot together is a victory of feeling over artifice and circumstance.

For example, when Helga and Peter met in a botany class, they were each fully involved in their own lives—he as a carpenter and she as a bookkeeper. But their interest in plants drew them together, and eventually they decided to go into partnership in a mail-order orchid business. Together, they created a new plot about success in a new business, in which each played an equal role.

Your goal in plot making should be to have as many fully dimensional characters as reasonably possible. This is a movement toward seeing people as ends rather than means, and allows no room for props or trophies. Fully dimensional characters retain the capacity to surprise and delight you (or infuriate you) just by being who they are. The shortest route to characterization like this is to read others, and love others, accurately—not for your idea of them or how they serve some image you have of yourself, but for themselves alone.

Exercises for Chapter 6

Summarizing and Selecting

Think about an event, decision, or experience of some importance: why you left a job; how your last romantic relationship ended; how you decided to live in the city (or small town, or suburb) in which you presently live.

1. In your notebook, write three *true but different* versions of the event. Notice which details you have selected for each story, and which you have chosen to leave out.
2. Why did you include some details and omit others—that is, what aspects of your character did you decide to emphasize at the expense of others?

Defensive Strategies

Focus on a situation in your life that makes you feel extremely vulnerable, perhaps because of a fear of judgment or rejection (for example, speaking in front of a large group, or disagreeing with your boss). Scrutinize the ways you try to hide your feelings of vulnerability.

1. List them in your notebook, being as specific as possible. These are your *defensive strategies*. Although they offer you a way to feel less fearful, you pay a high price for them because they limit your plot possibilities.
2. Now make a list of the ways that such defensive strategies close down your plot options. What do these strategies prohibit you from doing? Include small things, not just big dreams that you can't make come true. (For example, being afraid of looking silly means not only that you will never give a stirring speech before thousands of cheering people, but that you will never learn to ride a bicycle as an adult.)

Redescription

Choose an event, experience, or situation from your own life that took place in the last five years, and that you thought of as a central failure. Write a paragraph that redescribes it as an episode, showing how it functioned in your plot as a stepping stone or link.

Subplots

Identify three or more experiences in your life that have a common theme and list them. For example, you may find a set of commonly accepted ideas about when "more is better." This conventional story line says that staying in a comfortable, low-stress, nonprestigious job means that you are not realizing your potential by moving up to a more stressful, ambitious career; that a committed relationship, to be a solid one, must lead to living together, then marriage; and that this relationship may begin in separate rented apartments but must eventually lead to joint acquisition of residential property. A default story line indicates the presence of a subplot.

Hidden Instructions

Listen for the hidden instructions in people's stories. Choose three familiar stories that your mother or some other close relative or your best friend or mate tells. Tell each of them in a separate paragraph, and read them for themes.

1. How does each of their stories reveal the way its narrator sees the world? Dangerous? Beautiful? Logical? Completely random? Out of control?
2. How does each narrator cast himself or herself in relation to other people?
3. Embedded in their hidden instructions, are there clues to you about what roles this person would like you to play in their life?

Projection

1. Choose someone from your cast of characters about whom you have a strong feeling—fear, admiration, envy, and so on. Think about an incident between you and that person that brought out those feelings strongly (the time you thought your friend was snubbing you at a party, the time you thought your mother was selfish for wanting to take up so much of your time). Describe the incident in a paragraph.
2. Read the story and ask yourself if those feelings really belong to that person or if they emanate from you. Can you find in the other person's behavior some unappealing part of yourself, or some unacknowledged part of yourself that you long to be? Can you remember a time when you acted in a similar fashion?

Splitting

Most people appear to us to be more than one person—the person who loves soap operas and the person who reads poetry, and the person who plays pinball until midnight; the concerned parent and the free spirit who loves bungee jumping.

1. Choose a person from your cast of characters and describe two situations in which he or she acted like two different people.
2. Choose another person from your cast of characters. Describe a way he or she acted in one situation that obliterated how you had understood his or her character up until that point. Tell a new story that integrates both parts of that person's character.

Recasting and Rewriting Your Cast of Characters

Try to find three people in your cast of characters who have changed from one role to another in your life, but are still important in a positive way. Write their names, their old role, and their new role. (For example: Jack was my friend and is now my lover; Beverly was my next door neighbor and is now my mentor.)

1. Look for a common theme or element in your dealings with them that may have facilitated their transition from one role to the other (for example, you spent a lot of time in conversation with them).
2. Now find three people in or out of your cast of characters who no longer play roles in your life. Do they have anything in common? Would you like to include them in your plot, recast in a new role? What images of them (or

yourself) do you have to give up or change to find a new place for them in your life?

Your Many Roles

Go through your cast of characters and list as many of the roles you have played with each of them as far as you can. Be honest; some may be roles you're not too proud of. But keep in mind that the more roles you have played, both good and bad, the more you have in common with other people. Examples might include: friend, lover, mentor, martyr, teacher, parent, fool, seducer, betrayer, tattletale, creator, employee, rescuer, rebel, victim, clown, dictator, provider, dependent, caretaker, ally, enemy, expert, novice, seeker—the list is virtually endless.

Now look at your list. Does it show any pattern of diversity and variety? If not—if, for example, you have almost invariably played the role of caretaker—your plot is definitely in danger of becoming flat.

Write down some new roles you would like to see on your list, and reflect on how you might begin to write them.

Evolving Roles

List your three closest relationships in your current life:

1. Identify your current role in each
2. Identify the other person's current role
3. How has your role changed over time?
4. How has the other person's role changed over time?
5. How, in the future, would you like your role to change with this person? Would you like to cast yourself in some new additional roles?
6. How, in the future, would you like to change this per-

son's role in your life? Would you like to cast this person in some new additional roles?

Reading Character Through Action

Think of an incident in your life that you would label a "moment of truth"—a time when you were called on to take action, large or small—and write about what you did. (For example, you hit a car in a parking lot and fled without leaving a note.) How did your action or lack of action reveal your character? Did your actions surprise you pleasantly or unpleasantly?

Write a scene based on a real incident of conflict between you and your lover or close friend that reveals in a new way something about your lover's or close friend's character. How did their action or lack of action reveal their character? Did it surprise you pleasantly or unpleasantly?

Revising Your Read on a Character

Look at your cast of characters and find one about whom you have had to radically revise your opinion. (For example, Minnie seemed sweet and thoughtful when you first met, but now she seems insulting, spiteful, and untrustworthy.)

1. Write a line or two describing your first impression, and a line or two describing your current impression. Consider the two descriptions, and think about what connects the two.
2. Can you redescribe her in a way that merges the two impressions in a meaningful way?

7

Looking for Love in
All the Wrong Places:
Plots in Popular Culture

We are good at opening dialogue
It's our specialty
That and the goodbye scene
we could recite in our sleep.
It's the middle that defies us,
the substance, the ordinary progressions
that weave events into patterns,
textures, the three dimensional . . .
                              —Kate Braverman,
                              "Afterthoughts"

Ideally, our plot ideas should spring from the
wants and needs of our authentic self. When we are looking
outside ourselves for structure, however, we grab our plot
ideas from the nearest handy source. For most people, that
means modeling their lives on characters in TV and movies,
the messages embodied in popular songs, the books we read,

and the perceived lives of celebrities and friends. The result is that we continually strive to achieve the unattainable: a plot with a beginning, a middle, and a quick and happy resolution.

Plots from Popular Culture

Although viewers look for themselves in movies and TV, they are unlikely to find stories about how people like themselves live their lives. In fact, if someone deliberately set out to create images that would make us discontented with our lot, the result might be exactly the images we see. Unfortunately, there seems to be a direct relationship between how passively or unconsciously we accept plots and how clichéd and self-defeating they are.

Many people get their plot ideas from images of family relationships in movies, TV, and popular songs. When a certain kind of plot takes up a lot of space in the culture—the idea, for example, that the nuclear family can solve any problem life sends its way (and in half an hour!), or that true love vanquishes all obstacles—we tend to understand significant parts of ourselves in terms of these stories. When we compare these stories about intimate and family relationships to our own relationships, and we inevitably find ours wanting, our own lives become less real to us than what we see on the screen.

People want to know about others' relationships as a way to gauge and assess what's going on in their own, and movies and TV allow the viewer a chance to imaginatively enter other people's lives and see how they do relationships. In real life, the nuts and bolts of people's relationship plots are private and ultimately inaccessible to others. Sexual plots, about which we are intensely curious, are usually the most secret. In the world of TV and movies, however, the sexual plots are the most frequent and the most openly expressed.

The stories in pop culture moralize with such messages as

"Justice will triumph," "Having a baby cements a marriage," "Love can cure anyone of anything." At the same time, pop culture gives us externalized images of success, concentrating on material contentment at the expense of internal contentment, and idealizes sexual love.

Popular culture is a criticism of the self. It denigrates the realness of everyday life—real possibilities and difficulties, real bodies and faces. What it chooses to highlight makes it more than just a foreshortening of reality. It trades in clichés that are impossible to live up to: for both women and men, the impossible but glamorous image is of "having it all," of being married, having children, and succeeding in a high-powered career. To support these notions, the media have tended to portray single mothers as downtrodden and single women as desperate to get married, as if to say that if women don't opt for marriage and kids, woe betide them.

These images have grown so out of step with the realities of most people's lives that a greater realism has finally begun to intrude. No longer do the media—especially TV—persist in portraying the sitcom-style nuclear family, à la Ozzie and Harriet or Donna Reed, as the ideal; newer programs, such as *Grace Under Fire,* portray single-parent families, especially women, raising their children alone. But despite such iconoclastic TV families as the dysfunctional Connors in *Roseanne,* the classic nuclear family as depicted in early sitcoms has passed into our national mythos.

The sitcom has a basic plot structure that firmly supports the nuclear family and specific ways of resolving discord within it. From early sitcoms like *Father Knows Best* on through *The Cosby Show,* millions of viewers have learned how the family is supposed to work. As Gerard Jones writes in *Honey, I'm Home,* his study of sitcoms:

> Domestic harmony is threatened when a character develops a desire that runs counter to the group's welfare, or misunderstands a situation because of poor communication, or contacts

a disruptive outside element. The voice of the group—usually the voice of the father or equivalent chief executive—tries to restore harmony but fails, and the dissenter grabs at an easy, often unilateral solution. The solution fails, and the dissenter must surrender to the group for rescue. The problem turns out to be not very serious after all, once everyone remembers to communicate and surrender his or her selfish goals. The wisdom of the group and its executive is proved. Everyone, including the dissenter, is happier than at the outset.

Furthermore, the solution is arrived at in thirty to sixty minutes, and without recourse to anyone outside the family. The notions of problems too stubborn or complex for the group and its chief executive to solve, or of the embeddedness of group members in a life outside the group, never impinges on the standard sitcom plot. Achievements of family members must be brought back to the group and subjected to its approval. The false family of the sitcom is dangerously isolated—we never see the family members stray far outside their house, either literally or figuratively.

The deeper message of television is passivity. In contrast to radio or written text, TV doesn't require you to imagine anything; the images come into your home. Because you watch in comparative privacy, it encourages a kind of voyeurism. TV offers you a window in, permitting you to see into other people's lives without disclosing your own. You never have to be responsible for your reactions. TV gives the illusion of companionship—for example, meeting regularly at a bar like Cheers, "where everybody knows your name." But in reality, no one is meeting you; your rendezvous is with images in a box. You know *their* names; they don't know yours. You feel like you're in their house, but they're in your house. It's a false intimacy and false companionship.

We get some of our notions about men's relationship plots from male songwriters, especially those who write rock and roll and country and western songs. They appeal to women by presenting themselves as sensitive, vulnerable, and loyal. In *Female Desires,* Rosalind Coward notes:

> The lyrics reveal men time and time again speaking and singing and indeed thinking in ways that contradict how men present themselves outside the lyrics of pop songs. Here are men helplessly passionate, endlessly vulnerable, constant in love even in the face of insuperable odds. Here are men inconsolable and heartbroken, and men sensitive and gentle in their seductions—strange when we ponder on how often women bemoan men's often callous attitude to sex, men's insensitivity within relationships and men's lack of constancy in love.

Some rock and roll songs, of course, are simply male sexual braggadocio. But when the subject of the song is a relationship, the men are depicted as variously driven by guilt, shame, and loss; appealing to a woman for a second chance; assuring her of undying love; or revealing their innermost thoughts and reflections on the relationship—all in ways that are not common practice outside of song lyrics.

The images of men in rock and roll are subversive because they make women less content with the men they're with. Women assume that such sensitivity, devotion, and openness about emotions are available if they could just find the right man, or the right pathway into the heart of the man they already have. As the late Frank Zappa said, "The amount of damage that has been done over the years by love songs is incalculable."

Before the advent of TV's simple solutions in the fifties, many people took their plots from the melodramas they watched in the movies. These larger-than-life images were sometimes overpowering; and although they lacked the intimacy of television, many moviegoers were stirred to action or reduced to tears. Woody Allen's *Purple Rose of Cairo,* in which the hero of the silver screen literally leaps from the screen and into a real woman's life, is perhaps the ultimate moviegoer's fantasy. Now that we can bring movies into our homes via our VCRs and play our favorite scenes over and over again, their plots may have an even bigger impact than they once did.

TV, movies, and rock and roll all provide a window into relationships. Viewers and listeners compare their relationships, sometimes unconsciously, with what they see in these media and make assessments about their own intimate connections. These observed plots often appear more real than one's own life precisely because they *are* observed. Their inherent structures are more shapely—they have a beginning, middle, and end—and their dramatic foreshortening of time makes the impossible seem possible.

For example, when the movie *Pretty Woman* came out, I was amazed to discover how many of my female clients took it seriously. That version of the Cinderella fantasy—poor, beautiful, sweet woman meets rich, handsome man; they fall in love; he showers her with luxurious gifts; they live happily ever after—made them feel as though they were deprived in their ordinary struggles and relationships.

On the other hand, it is possible to be positively influenced by movies. Tania remembers how seeing the movie *Out of Africa* in high school changed her life. She had grown up in a small town in the Midwest and had never traveled anywhere. Her mother and her three sisters and their families all lived in the same town, and they were a very close extended family. Tania went to see *Out of Africa* five times, and was enchanted by the portrayal of Isak Dinesen, the Danish woman who moved to Africa, ran a farm, and lived an interesting life. The story stayed with her to such a degree that after high school, she joined the Peace Corps and went to Africa, where she eventually settled.

Clearly, plots from popular culture provide powerful—and often destructive—templates for our own lives. We therefore need to be careful consumers of popular culture and to learn to recognize when the messages it transmits have something to do with reality and are meaningful to us and when they don't.

Fictional Plots

Novels give us some of the best examples of complex and subtle information, unfolded over time, about other people. Good fiction offers three things to the plot maker that are offered nowhere else: the example of a more nuanced plot; access to the inner workings of the narrator; and an experiential relationship to the element of time, because reading a novel takes time.

In contrast to the passive receiver of TV and movies, the reader of a novel has an ongoing experience that requires *active* use of the imagination. At times, when you are engrossed in a good novel, the imaginary world becomes all-encompassing, intimate, and real, while your everyday life recedes far away.

Cervantes's *Don Quixote* provides the classic model of the overinvolved reader, as Theodore Sarbin explains in his essay "A Root Metaphor":

> One of the most illuminating models for the formation of the self-narrative is the protagonist of Cervantes's novel, *Don Quixote.* From reading of adventure tales about chivalric characters, Don Quixote constructed an identity for himself and a corresponding narrative plot in which to act out his role. [The literary critic Harry] Levin has assigned the label, the Quixotic principle, to the frequently observed practice of a reader building an identity and a self-narrative from reading books.

This multifaceted, multitextured, private experience of reading evokes a complex emotional and intellectual response from the reader. If you can learn about plotting from anywhere, it should be here.

Consider a book written in the first person, in which you have total access to the narrator. Here you get the narrator's thoughts and perceptions first-hand, and see how they shape his tale. You see his struggle close up and understand, with greater sympathy, the cause-and-effect relationship between his character and the events that befall him. For example, in *The Catcher in the Rye*, Holden Caulfield draws us into his mind from the very first line: "If you really want to hear about it, the first thing you'll probably want to know is where I was born, what my lousy childhood was like, and how my parents were occupied and all before they had me, and all that David Copperfield kind of crap, but I don't really feel like going into it, if you want to know the truth." We, as readers, are hooked by the intimacy and idiosyncrasy of Holden—we feel we really know him.

Unless we have tremendous psychic abilities, only passionate love and great literature give us the opportunity to enter the mind of a narrator other than ourselves. As Ethel Person suggests:

> Perhaps the reason that fiction has so successfully claimed love as its province is that fiction and love—at their respective best—do something similar: they enable their adherents (readers and lovers) to enter into another consciousness. In the case of fiction, the consciousness entered is, most immediately, that of the character through whose eyes we are seeing events, but ultimately it is that of the author. In love the consciousness we share is that of our beloved.

In novels with third-person narrators, like those of Jane Austen or George Eliot, you as the reader are offered a point of view that you can never have about your own life. Exposure to this all-seeing view gives us the opportunity to think how our own behavior might appear to wise and perceptive others. Of course, this an unattainable ideal since no one, including a writer, can be completely objective about life.

The primary difference between plot in fiction and plot in life is that *there is no conclusive resolution in life.* Plot in fiction, of necessity, has a beginning, a middle, and an end. Plot in life, however, has only tentative endings because the narrator is always changing, however subtly, and there is always life ahead to be lived. (For those who believe in past lives, plot possibilities are even further extended.) As contemporary philosopher Richard Rorty puts it, "It is . . . hard to imagine a human life which felt itself complete, a human being who dies happy because all that he or she ever wanted has been attained." As long as the narrator is interested in enlarging a sense of wonder, understanding, and solidarity with others, the story continues to be complicated and beautiful.

Another common error we make is to assume that time unfolds in life as it does in art. We forget that much of life is unplottable. As we have seen, your plot usually consists less of what actions you plan than how you play the cards life deals you.

Most of life—real life—is not dramatic. As we will see in a later chapter, however, the plots we see in fiction, theater, TV, and movies lead us to believe that life is fraught with tension and drama because they show us characters at the crossroads of their lives. Fortunately or not, the dross of life—boredom and routine, endless arguing, planning dinner night after night, going to bed on time, making the same mistake over and over—takes up most of our time.

Fiction, whether it is a great novel or a trashy soap opera, seduces us into believing that our narratives, too, can share their structure, time sense, and resolution. To accept this is to miss one of the great differences between art and life, and to cheat yourself when writing your own plot. Some processes, like the deepening of a friendship or marriage, or the growth of mastery in a skill or discipline, cannot be sped up. Key moments in the process can be picked out, but its unfolding in real time cannot be hurried. Art gives us myriad insights into

life, but it deceives us in this: it excludes everything that ac-
crues or ripens slowly, in imperceptible stages.

Life Stories of the Rich and Famous

We can't seem to help comparing our lives to those of
celebrities, who always appear to have more and better than we
can hope for. Stars' personal lives are chronicled in magazines
like *Vanity Fair* and *People*. Publications like these attempt to
make celebrities seem more human, more approachable, and—
underneath the veneer of glamour—just like us, but this impression of humanity is carefully stage managed. Stars aren't
just regular folks, and they are not our friends, no matter how
many personal details we read about them. What we see of
them is not their intimate reality and thus is a kind of fraudulent plot in the sense that it is consciously created for the public's consumption. Such pseudo-confessional stories carefully
select how a star is portrayed.

Usually, their fictionalized family life—the one they want
their fans to believe—is very different from the reality of their
sexual nature and choice of partners. The last twenty years
have shown us many examples of this, two of the most noto-
rious being the dichotomy between the heterosexual sex symbol image of Rock Hudson and his real-life death from AIDS
and consequent exposure of his bisexual identity; and O. J.
Simpson's nice-guy image blown to smithereens with his being tried for the murders of his ex-wife and her friend and the
ensuing explosive revelations about his personal life. Even earlier in the century, C. G. Jung kept his sexual life and his work
separate in the eyes of the public, though they were deeply in-
tertwined in private. He omitted mention of Antonia Wolff
from his autobiography, although she had been his therapist
as well as his mistress for over thirty years.

Why are we so entranced by celebrities, whom we know in

our hearts to be human beings, just like us? John Ellis, a professor of film studies, explains:

> Stars have a soldering function: they hold the news and the personal together by being both public and intimate, by being news only in so far as they are persons. . . . Stars are incomplete images outside the cinema . . . at once ordinary and extraordinary, available for desire and unattainable. . . . Star images are paradoxical. They are composed of clues rather than complete meanings, of representations that are less complete, less stunning than those offered by cinema.

From stars' images, we get a vision of godlike, graceful beings in a dramatic and meaningful world; further, because we believe that inside they're like us, we get the idea that this perfected world can be ours if we have good looks, wealth, and fame.

Celebrities often function as role models or at least signposts of possibilities along the highway of life. They seem to beckon, embodying a world of ageless beauty, limitless luxury, impeccable taste, and lavishly rewarded talent. Yet according to magazines and newspapers, deep inside they are just like us. Celebrities' lives, as portrayed by the media, shape our expectations about how life works. Celebrities always embody the quality of glamour. Glamour has transformative power— we tend to feel that if we had it, our lives would be wonderful—and this desire for transformation is linked to one of the major plot complications, escape. Celebrities also serve as channels for our resentment. We like to see the proud and mighty fall; we take pleasure sometimes in the distress of others, especially if we envied their good fortune.

The star portrait, carefully edited and refined, calculated to support and enhance his or her career by extending "starring roles" beyond the realm of film, has nothing to do with a real plot. Regarding the fiction of celebrities' lives, the critic Neil Gabler coined the phrase "life movie, " which is neither a life nor a movie:

When life itself is an entertainment medium it also forces adjustments from the stars of films, TV, records and the rest of the conventional media. . . . Elizabeth Taylor . . . may be as close to a theorist of the life movie as there is. . . . [Her] life was so much more entertaining that anything she could do on screen that she didn't have to work in movies or TV to hold our interest. She just had to live. . . . Elizabeth Taylor understood that one could keep unraveling the long skein of one's life; that one makes of one's life a movie. . . . Lives have themes as well as plots, and these themes can be a major part of their appeal: the content that informs the story. One of the appeals of Elizabeth Taylor's life is that it forcefully conveys the theme of survival. No matter what happens to Liz, she triumphs.

Neil Gabler offers a vignette that illustrates how we use each other as props or walk-ons:

In *Truth or Dare,* Kevin Costner saunters backstage to pay his respects [to Madonna] after a concert. Flashing that big lopsided Costner grin, he tells her the concert was "neat," then apologizes for having to get back home to the kids. No sooner has Mr. Costner left than Madonna is sneering incredulously, "Neat?" and sticking her finger down her throat to gag. Madonna didn't seem to realize that she had momentarily become a guest star in Mr. Costner's life movie, believing instead that he was a guest star in hers. "Neat" was deliberate and probably ironic. It is the sort of thing one expects Mr. Costner to say. And the excuse about getting back to the children is . . . central to the Costner "movie."

This is a stunning example of the fraudulence of the "life movie" of celebrities. Madonna's concert had certainly not ended before eleven P.M.—when Costner's children were surely long asleep. This is a classic example of how we as viewers are asked to believe that we are taken into stars' private lives and are garnering a glimpse of their private realities, but in truth we are *really* taken in—that is, deceived: Costner's children were functioning as props buttressing his preferred public role as devoted father, which was blown apart in 1994 by his separation and exposure as a womanizer.

. . . and Not so Rich and Famous

When we draw our plot possibilities from our understanding of our friends' and acquaintances' plots, we engage in another kind of fictionalization. People exchange details of their intimate lives with their friends. We gauge our own lives against what we think is going on in theirs. For example, "*She* got a box of chocolates for Valentine's Day, why didn't I?" "Mike's wife doesn't complain about giving him oral sex, why should mine?"

While people are in a love affair, they like to feel it is seamless. When it ends, they reveal the rips and snags or gaping holes that happened along the way. We create fictions about marriage and family—certainly for others' benefit, but often for ourselves as well. We always present an *image* of our relationships based on what we prefer others to see. We talk easily about gifts given and received, dinners out, vacations that we're planning. But when we do speak truthfully about difficulties in our relationships, the struggles and betrayals and disappointments, we often feel we are betraying our partners. In this way the relationship plots of friends—while apparently the most truthful and reliable source of plot information—are often the most fraudulent.

We listen to stories of others' lives to figure out how to assess our own. We don't know how much sex is supposed to be satisfying, how much money is generous, and so forth, so we often size up our lives in comparison to others' in order to be able to ask for more of what we want or to reassure ourselves that what we have is enough. Hearing that other people have problems, too, is comforting, so often we tend to idealize the lives of others and denigrate our own, because we are so much more familiar with our own problems.

The next time you find yourself rhapsodizing over how much better your friend's life is than yours, engage your friend in conversation and perform a reality check. For example, Dana envied Vera her chocolates on Valentine's Day because Dana's husband couldn't even remember what day it was. But when Dana commented on this to Vera, she discovered that Vera thought her husband was incredibly insensitive—after all, he should know that she's worried about her weight and would much prefer a nonfood gift!

Exercises for Chapter 7

Plots from Music

List three love songs that have been your "favorites" at various times in your life. Describe the "plots" of each, and why it seemed meaningful to you at the time. (For example, here's the plot of "The Tennessee Waltz": A man is dancing with his lover to a favorite song, when another man cuts in and takes his girlfriend for good. Every time he hears that song he misses his girlfriend even more.)

1. First, go over the list to see if the songs have a common theme. Do you like songs about unrequited love? True love? Powerful women? Loners?
2. Now pick one of these songs, and write a few lines describing what you were doing at the time it was meaningful to you (breaking up with a lover, studying for exams, working late every night, being pregnant) and how the song made you feel then. Did you wish your life could be like the song? Did the song make you feel better or worse about your life?
3. How do you feel about this song now?

Plots from Movies

List your three favorite movies, and write a brief synopsis of the plot and characters.

1. With which characters did you identify (the poor girl who was saved by the rich man, the heroine with the machine gun, the guy who never got the girl, the traveling loner who broke hearts in every town)?
2. Can you identify a connecting theme?
3. Write a few lines describing the impact of these characters on your life. (Are you always wistful because your life is not as romantic as your movie? Do you wish your own life was as exciting as your favorite thriller? Are you disappointed because your mate is not like the romantic lead in the movie?)

Literature

Choose a book that you have read and enjoyed.

1. What character did you identify with?
2. What does this say about the way you see the world?
3. If you had written the book, would you have changed anything about your character's life?

Optional: choose a book that you and your partner have both read and enjoyed.

1. Which character did you identify with?
2. Which character did your mate identify with?
3. What does this say about the differences or similarities in the way you each see the world?
4. Did you feel that this book described something about your relationship?

Celebrity Role Models

Think of a celebrity, dead or alive, who has served as a role model, or at least whom you have found extremely interesting.

1. Describe him or her as an ordinary person.
2. Describe the person as the opposite sex. What kind of life would he or she have lived?
3. What kind of life would the person have had if he or she lived in a different era?
4. What compliment does this person really need to hear that he or she never does?
5. What does this person need to cry about?
6. Imagine that you have suddenly became very famous, and are a celebrity yourself. Who do others think you are? Are you the same person, or have you changed? What do you think of the other celebrities you meet?

8

On the Road: How Plots Change

The power of redescribing, the power of language to make new and different things possible and important—an appreciation which becomes possible only when one's aim becomes an expanding repertoire of alternative descriptions rather than The One Right Description.

—Richard Rorty,
*Contingency, Irony
and Solidarity*

A wonderful difference between fiction and real life is that, unlike fictional characters, who are at the whim of their author, we do not have to be stuck in a predetermined plot. Once we learn to take hold of the narrative reins, we can create new plots for ourselves. When we learn to recognize what plot we're enacting, where it comes from, and how we have assigned roles to ourselves and others, we can begin to make new choices and take different actions that will propel us onto a different track.

Understanding how plot works can help us create, defend, maintain, redefine, and refine our identity. It also permits us to assimilate experiences into our continuing narrative without forever starting from scratch. Without a plot, we would be like people who suffer long-term memory loss: everything would seem to be happening to us as if for the first time, and we would never have the chance to examine and learn from our experiences.

Plot keeps life interesting. It's a way to stay present in life, to keep reflecting on past events and anticipating new ones: "Leaving that last job was hard, but I know I can do better. I can't wait to find out what my next job will be." Plot can even allow us the luxury of seeing our life as part of some fictional genre: a detective story, an erotic novel, a quest, a romance, in which we can cast ourselves as the hero or heroine. Plotting lets us embellish, dramatize, express ourselves, reinterpret key experiences, try out new identities and roles, and spot unforeseen ways to enliven our existence. As fiction writer Alice Munro said in an interview, "Cherished beliefs change. Ways of dealing with life change. All this seems to me endlessly interesting. . . . If you find life interesting, it just goes on being so. . . . If you find something interesting—really interesting—it's very hard to regret it! You may think, Oh, that was frivolous behavior, and that was selfish behavior, and that was perhaps damaging behavior—but wasn't it interesting! . . . Regret fades away in the face of interest."

Plot charts development and change. Take a moment to think about your plot as you might have recounted it to a stranger on a plane just after your college graduation. You were free to portray yourself in any way you chose, and you had reached a milestone in your life without in any way exhausting your possibilities. How would you have described your accomplishments and plans, portrayed your character and tastes?

Sometimes we don't realize that we have changed until we start to tell a familiar version of our plot and find that it doesn't sound right anymore. For example, Joanie was a brilliant student. She blazed through graduate school and became the youngest microbiologist ever hired at her university. As a consequence, despite her intellect and accomplishments, she had always seen herself as a youthful outsider. But at age forty, she was jolted into a completely different perspective when she suddenly found herself being asked for advice by graduate students, and looked up to for her knowledge and years of experience.

In a sense, we split into two selves when we describe our experiences: the one who speaks, and the one who listens and judges the appropriateness of the description. For years Fred described himself as shy, and he was quiet and reserved all through high school. But one night at a party, he suddenly heard himself telling a story to a complete stranger about what a ham he was in his improvisational theater class. After that, he could no longer tell the story about what a shy person he was, and he was forced to reevaluate his plot.

In our storytelling, we become both writer and reader, speaker and listener, observer and actor, and we adjust our narrative to balance the two competing sets of demands. For example, what feels right to the speaker may sound melodramatic or whining to the listener, so as we relate the story we tone it down a bit.

Powerful Plots

Some plots seem to be so powerful that they create themselves over and over, and you fear you will never be able to change them. In truth, some plots are more difficult to revise than others. For example, the plot of the abused child who grows up to find abusive lovers or to abuse others exerts a very strong undertow. The plot of addiction is also extremely powerful. These strong plots seem to have the pull of gravity, and can drag even the most resolute characters in their wake. It takes a strong, self-aware character to take apart their machinery and put it back together in a new form, and it may be difficult to rescue yourself from such a plot without help.

Not all powerful plots are so negative, however. Raising a child is a strong plot, for example, because it gives form to your life. You can't decide to feed the baby tomorrow instead of right now, nor can you simply walk out of the house whenever you feel like it. You can rewrite the plot so that you don't act like a martyr about caring for the child, but you can't write the child out of the plot unless you want your story to include going to jail! Another example of a strong plot is that of romance, with its many clichéd subplots and characters: the triangle, the unrequited love, the femme fatale, the star-crossed lovers. As we have seen, these plots tend to follow a predictable course and to offer only constricting roles.

Sometimes it is our unexamined assumptions about life that do us in: the idea that long-term relationships inevitably become stale or humdrum; that living with a teenager is hell; that life goes downhill after forty. It is very important to look at seldom-examined ideas like these. To creatively rewrite our narratives, we need all the freedom to redescribe our lives that we can get. Weeding out assumptions of this kind gives us more freedom to use poetic license when writing our plots.

For example, Mark, sixty, worked as a tax accountant all his life. He and his wife, Grace, had been married for thirty-five years and were devoted to each other. They led a quiet, peaceful life, enjoying their shared interest in literature and classical music. When Grace died of cancer after several years of home care, Mark was devastated and exhausted. He accepted as a given that he would spend what remained of his life living quietly, alone in the small house they had shared. He worked more hours to fill the void Grace had left, and spent his free time reading and watching TV.

After two years of this solitary life, some old friends introduced him to Francine, a woman his own age who had been widowed for ten years. Francine was nothing like Grace. She was passionate about life, and loved to travel and go to flea markets. Mark was enchanted by her energy. He had always thought of himself as a stay-at-home kind of guy who considered travel too much trouble and expense. But listening to Francine describe her trips to London each year, and the wonderful plays she saw and the interesting things she found at the outdoor markets, made him rethink his assumptions. The quiet retirement he'd envisioned was looking less and less interesting. He took a deep breath and decided to open himself up to new adventures. He and Francine became a couple, and what Mark had assumed would be a limited retirement punctuated by his own inevitable decline and death turned into something completely different.

What are some of your own assumptions? Here are some common ones: "You should stay married for life—divorce is an admission of failure." "People who vote differently from me are basically immoral." "If you disagree with your parents, you're being disrespectful." It may be difficult at first to discern your assumptions; you are searching for unconsciously held beliefs that you accept to such a degree that they have become the wallpaper of your life.

Movement in Plot: How We Get from A to Z

Unlike novels and plays, which have chapters and acts, plots in our lives unfold by increments that are difficult to identify. We may not realize how we got from point A to point G—from wanting to apprentice yourself to your mentor to wanting to buy him a one-way ticket to Tierra del Fuego—but a progression of some kind obviously took place. You may say, "I can't understand how I wound up sleeping with her," but your office mate did not simply pole-vault across the desk into your lap—hard as the steps from small talk to liking to nascent desire to invitation to acceptance may be to identify. By the same logic, you did not go from wanting to play guitar in a rock and roll band to hanging out your shingle as a certified public accountant in one or two simple steps.

To see how plots unfold in fiction, let's look at Edgar G. Ulmer's 1945 *noir* film, *Detour*. In this film, an impoverished pianist hitchhiking across the country to join his fiancée accepts a ride from a motorist. During a thunderstorm, far from any help, the motorist dies of heart failure. The pianist, fearful of being disbelieved by the authorities, takes the motorist's identification and cash and continues west, leaving his own identification and clothes on the corpse. He picks up a woman hitchhiker at a filling station, only to discover that she knew the dead motorist and plans to blackmail him unless he helps her claim the man's insurance. In a nightmarish twist, he inadvertently strangles her with a telephone cord as she attempts to call the police to turn him in. Now he can be convicted of two murders—including, ironically, his own, since he has assumed the other man's identity. In a series of small decisions, the pianist's life is plotted from A to Z, each step further reducing his freedom, but all stemming from the seemingly trivial decision to accept a ride in that car and no other.

In real life, steps are rarely this clear. One action plots another, and not all of these actions are under your control. You may think of step 10 only as a consequence of step 9, but step 10 couldn't have been an option unless step 2 had led to steps 3, 4, 5, and so on. To understand how you got where you are, it is important to look back at all the steps that contributed to the outcome, always keeping in mind that it may take some investigation to identify where this plot, or the larger pattern of which it forms a part, actually began.

Sophie was a photographer when she met Andy, an architect. Although she did some commercial work for ad agencies, she was most interested in trying to put together a body of her photographic collages that she could make into a show and book. Andy found a rundown Victorian house that they could buy and fix up and live in, and have a rental unit as well. They pooled their money and borrowed from family and moved in to begin serious renovation. Andy began to be obsessed with the construction work. Inevitably, things went wrong and cost more than he had anticipated. They had to borrow more money, and Andy asked Sophie to put her collage work aside and take more commercial jobs. Feeling under pressure, Sophie looked for advertising jobs, but they were getting hard to find. Finally, she saw an ad for a photographer to take school pictures, and she applied for and got the job. It was a long commute to the different schools in the area, the hours were long, and the work was not satisfying creatively, but the job was secure and they needed the money. Too exhausted to continue with her own work, Sophie began to wonder how she had gotten so far from her original goals.

Plot, ultimately, reveals character. The things that happen to us are not as important as how we respond to them. How you handle the daily choices life presents you with decides your character and determines your fate much more than what you plan to do or be. Taking responsibility for our part in such chains of events helps solve some of these mysteries. However, it is too simplistic to speak of motive or premeditation in, for example, the erosion of a marriage or the deterioration of a friendship. Very little in life happens because someone sets out to accomplish a specific goal. It is rare for life to present us with choices in which the consequences of our actions are clear. The steps we take, especially in relation to other people, can be as insignificant as a glance or a touch, yet have far-reaching moral consequences.

The Plot of Noncommitment

As I pointed out earlier, your life will have a plot whether you choose it or not. Some people mistakenly think that they can keep all their options open forever simply by remaining uncommitted. But refusal to act is a plot in itself. For example, Francesca was something of a perfectionist. She didn't want to embarrass herself by choosing the wrong mate and having to get a divorce, and she was determined not to get married "until the right man comes along." As a consequence, she never got married. At forty-seven, she looks back wryly:

> Every man I went out with seemed to have a fatal flaw. George was argumentative, Paul was indecisive, and it was clear that Bobby would never make enough money. For some reason, I was really attractive to men, and I thought I had all the time in the world to make this decision. I thought the flow of men in my life would never stop. But that's not how life works. As I got older and more experienced, my criteria for the perfect man got narrower and narrower. Over the years, my options, which I thought would always remain open, became fewer and fewer. Now, finally, I'm sick of being alone. I can see that if I want to find a companion in life, I'm going to have to begin to accept people, warts and all. God knows, I've got my own problems!

While commitment closes off some options, it opens up others. Only by forsaking some plot options can depth in others be attained.

Marriage is the classic example of commitment. In marriage, two people make a commitment to stay together "for better or worse." You live with the person you married day in and day out—when you have the flu, when you have a bad hair day, when you can't stand your mate's taste in movies. As time passes and you continue to honor your commitment, through good times and bad, you have a chance to see what obstacles get in the way of your decision to stay together. You learn to identify, examine, understand, and ultimately conquer the parts of you that resist not only your resolution to remain a couple but other resolutions as well.

Noncommitment is also a plot. It may be a plot written in terms of perpetually starting over, or of vanishing when others start to depend on you. Perhaps the price you pay for retaining great freedom of action is never achieving or finishing anything. We all know people who are incapable of making a romantic commitment, so all their love relationships are brief, repetitive, and unfruitful. When you are stuck in a plot of avoidance that doesn't evolve into commitment you are limited to very few moves, like a person who can only go around in circles because one foot is nailed to the floor.

In short, the meter on plot is always running! You cannot escape plot by avoiding commitment or putting off composing your "real" life narrative. If life is what happens while you are making other plans, plot is what happens while you are doing the research for the "authorized" version of your life story.

Cultural Revisions

Certain plots happens on a cultural as well as an individual level. As anyone who lived through the sixties can tell you, when an entire culture looks for a way out of imposed parameters, all hell can break loose.

In the late sixties and early seventies, many assumptions about individual and social roles seemed to be up for renegotiation. It suddenly seemed imperative to question family, home, work, and love—to experiment with sexuality, lifestyle, drugs, dress, music, religion, and politics. During this exciting and adventurous time, the new cultural plot of revolution—of thinking the unthinkable and imagining the unimaginable—

blew up the seemingly immovable and basically conservative plots that had dominated people's lives for the previous two decades. Many young people began to question the assumptions that had so dominated their lives. They had sex before marriage and lived together without marrying, they had interracial relationships, they sought peace and love rather than money and success. Young people felt that the adult world had lost authenticity, and that their generation, which refused to comply with what it saw as corrupt systems of power, would define new values.

The plot of revolution is a peculiarly youthful one and depends to a large degree on the absolutism and idealism of youth. By the time we reach our thirties and forties, we have usually reached some kind of accommodation with the world and are less likely either to believe in a transfiguring principle or to put our lives on the line for it. It is no accident that the plot of "the sixties," with its contempt for the adult Establishment and its conviction that the way to right living would be found by the young, was written by those in their late teens and twenties. This attempt to throw out the existing plot and substitute a revolutionary one met with some success—our institutions and popular culture do reflect great changes effected during this time or as a result of pressure exerted then. But a plot of eternal questioning cannot be permanent.

Nor does true openness and flexibility mean merely substituting one plot for another. Throwing out the existing plot, as happened in the sixties, can be a disavowal of responsibility, a way of shirking onerous obligations, of not persevering when the going gets rough. Continually reinventing oneself to avoid going deeper into existing aspects of one's life is not what I mean by creative rewriting of your plot. In fact, it may mean that you have a deeper plot of dropping projects before completion or abandoning people before you meet your responsibilities toward them, perhaps in order to avoid being judged or hurt. Do not mistake the freedom to reinvent yourself for freedom from the responsibilities you yourself have created.

Constants and Variables

Even though you may want to throw out your entire plot and start all over again, some things just cannot be changed. Certain elements of life, such as your gender (unless you become a transsexual), ethnic group, parenthood, and so forth, are constants and are not susceptible to creative plotting. If you are a woman you can't write a plot in which you are a man, though you can certainly aspire to more careers and interests than your mother or grandmother could. If you are the father of a child, your plot cannot exclude this fact, although it may include your being an irresponsible parent if you refuse to accept the role.

Plotting is a continuous activity that is built on a relationship of past to future, so the elements you can change coincide with what you are able to foresee or predict. Experience leads us, sometimes reluctantly, to knowledge, and this knowledge can help us predict certain possibilities or outcomes. For example, if it's quite clear to you that everyone you sleep with turns out to be trouble, you can apply this useful rule to your sexual opportunities and begin trying to understand why it should be so. Asking yourself questions—How do I respond to sexual attention? How do I handle conflict? What do I do when confronted with a party of strangers? Why do people with scars on their faces turn me on?—can help you to see what your plot is. Repeatable events do lead to an understanding of patterns.

Connie, for example, always had a problem dealing with separation and distance. As a child she was frequently left with nannies, and every summer she was sent away to a distant camp where her parents never visited. She says:

> I was lonely for most of my life, so when someone I got involved with began to pull away, I'd do whatever I could to pull him back in—I'd cry, I'd beg, I'd tell him how much I needed

him and how much his leaving would hurt me. Of course, this charming behavior just made them run faster and farther. I can't tell you how many years it took me to figure it out. When I began to look at my life as narrative, I began to see that my plot was "Everyone I love always leaves me." Once I became aware of that, and my role in it, I was almost embarrassed. I knew you could change your plot by changing your actions, so I thought, okay, enough. I don't want that plot anymore. I decided that no matter what, no matter how much pain I was in, no matter how much I wanted to reach out and tie that person to the bed to keep them from leaving, I would just bite my tongue, sit on my dialing fingers, and let the person go. It was harder than hell, I'll tell you—my tongue was bitten to a bloody pulp. But it worked.

Connie's decision to revise her plot resulted in enormous changes. Some of the people who'd left missed her and came back, more people sought her out in the first place, and she felt exhilarated to be free of a painful and destructive pattern.

Lauren had a similar experience. She was often upset with her husband, Bill, because he was chronically late. No matter what time he said he would be somewhere, he was at least a half hour off. Sometimes she took his lateness as a personal insult, and other times she wondered why he just couldn't look at a watch and tell what time it was. Over the fifteen years of their marriage she had tried everything from threats to tears, and by the time they got to any event together, she was usually anxious and angry. Then one day she took at good look at her situation and realized that although she couldn't control Bill's lateness, she could predict it. Since she couldn't change his behavior, she changed her own. She realized that she could simply drive herself to events they were invited to, whether Bill was ready or not. This took the pressure off of Bill as well, and they were both able to enjoy engagements in fine spirits.

Take a few minutes to think about predictable outcomes in

your life that seem impervious to change. Are they really? Or is there some small action you can take that will redirect your plot in new and exciting ways?

Plot Breakers

As we have seen, some elements of plot are fixed, and some are changeable. Some, however, are unforeseeable: unplanned and unsought events that are frightening, magnificent, unthinkable. These plot breakers can rip into the fabric of your life and turn it inside out in an instant: a fire that burns down your house and robs you of security, a robbery on a dark street that shakes your feeling of safety, the sudden death of a close friend that reminds you of your own mortality, a spiritual vision that rocks your perceptions of the nature of life. These unpredictable, uncontrollable events turn your life upside down because nothing in your plot equips you to envision them.

Unplottable events are often considered to be luck, fate, or chance. You can claim little or no responsibility for these events. They cannot be planned for, and they recast forever the elements of your plot. Nor do they have any relation to character. You can be a good person and have good luck; you can be a mean, unscrupulous person and have good luck. You may discover buried treasure while walking on the beach, or chance upon a rapist at a dormitory mixer. (Although a divorce may be devastating for you, divorce is *not* an example of the unplottable because you have always had a hand in that plot.)

Serious illness, especially at the end of the twentieth century, is a plot breaker in the lives of more and more people. Dealing with illness is never pleasant or welcome, and it is never something we get because we deserve it. It can, however, present us with an important opportunity to revitalize our plots and our role as narrator. The literary critic Anatole Broyard, in his final book, *Intoxicated by My Illness,* writes about his experience with prostate cancer. He comments, "The patient has to start by treating his illness not as a disaster, an occasion for depression or panic, but as a narrative, a story. Stories are antibodies against illness and pain. . . . I sometimes think that silence can kill you . . . and I think that language, speech, stories, or narratives are the most effective way to keep our humanity alive." And in *A Whole New Life,* novelist Reynolds Price says, "Grieve for a decent limited time over whatever parts of your old self you know you'll miss. . . . Next find your way to be somebody else, the next viable you."

Since we tend to think we know what we are doing at all times—before the day begins we "know" that we're going to get up, eat breakfast, drive to work, get tired, come home, eat dinner, watch TV, and go to sleep—such unplottable events as illness and catastrophe create a substantive shift in our plots and our view of ourselves. They derail the old narrative and rip up the track it once ran on so smoothly.

Corrina, thirty-seven, was a psychologist on the staff of a teaching hospital. A single mother, she lived alone with her seven-year-old son. One evening, while she was driving home after dropping her son off at a slumber party, a man walked straight into the path of her car. She saw no one, but the loud thump of her car striking something was unmistakable. She stopped, went back, and found the body of a man lying in the middle of the street. The man was taken to the hospital. The police questioned her about the accident and let her go. Shattered, she went home, where her best friend, Nicole, took care of her. Early in the morning Nicole phoned the hospital and learned that the man had died during the night.

Corrina's world would never be the same again. At first, she was terrified that she would be sent to jail, and that everything she valued would be taken away from her. She feared that she would lose her child, her house, her garden, her work—that she would lose her mind. Three days later she was told that the man she had killed had been ill and disoriented for some time, and that no one considered the accident to be her fault. She would not go to jail, nor would her life change outwardly in any way. But from this experience she learned how fragile and impermanent life is—that truly, everything can change in a minute. She felt this realization not just intellectually but in every cell of her body.

This is a trauma. Trauma slices through your plot and labels everything on either side of it "before" or "since." Trauma calls upon the self in an either/or fashion: either you learn from it and broaden the self, or shrink from it and narrow the self. There is no middle ground, psychologically speaking. When you choose to face down trauma, you must rethink almost everything from the ground up; trauma shakes you to your foundations.

Not all plot breaking events are negative. You could win $20 million in the lottery. You could walk into a supermarket and fall completely, irreversibly in love with a man you meet in the checkout line. A mentor you haven't thought of in years could call you up and offer you a dream job in Paris.

Kenneth, forty-nine, had trouble with low self-esteem all his life. He had been stuck in a comfortable but poorly paid job in a bookstore, that wasn't really going anywhere. In his spare time he wrote novels and screenplays, none of which had been published. Then, as he says, "Lady luck stepped into my life."

> We held readings at the bookstore once a week—authors came to read passages of their books and sign copies for us to sell. One day a famous actress—a *really* famous actress—came to the store to discuss her new autobiography. I was going to introduce her, so we needed to spend some time talking about the book. I was nervous, but she turned out to be a fabulous person. Just a normal person. We really hit it off, and she asked me about myself. When she asked to see my screenplay, I thought, "What the hell, she's never going to read it,

but it's nice of her to ask." Well, to make a long story short, she read it and loved it and wanted to produce it. They had to scrape me off the floor, I was so happy.

In a matter of a few weeks, Kenneth's life had changed a hundred and eighty degrees. Agents and producers deluged him with phone calls, and he was given an enormous sum of money. After his initial elation, however, a surprising thing happened.

I was totally depressed. It suddenly hit me that I had wasted my whole life being passive and not pursuing my dreams. I couldn't adjust to being taken seriously by these movers and shakers. I still saw myself as this little guy who worked in a bookstore. To make it worse, a lot of my old friends rejected me. They told me I was selling out to Hollywood, but I know they just couldn't handle the fact that I was now this successful guy and their lives hadn't changed. But my life had changed, and I gradually began to realize that I was responsible not only for my past failures but for my success. I realized that the way I had seen myself had played an enormous role in the drab little life I had created.

Plot breakers, both positive and negative, have one element in common: they fundamentally threaten the sense of a coherent self. They are difficult or impossible to integrate into your plot because they call so much of what has preceded them into question. Although it may seem odd, many people have more trouble accepting wonderful news than catastrophic news, because like Kenneth they realize that they have made a huge investment of time, energy, and emotion in the wrong story. The new plot means that from now on they must get used to seeing themselves—and being seen by others—in a different way, one that's unfamiliar and harder to control.

Breaking the Pull of Inertia

As we have seen, certain elements in life are susceptible to plot revision and some are not. Between the two is a third force, inertia. While not as dramatic as life-changing trauma or accidents of birth, it can have a tremendous impact on the course of our plots.

Inertia is the enormous pull of the status quo, of habit, of what has already been set up in your life: a comfortable job that doesn't challenge you but isn't disagreeable enough to quit, or a marriage that isn't a deeply enriching connection but provides a framework for the rest of your life. You might not choose all these things or people over again, but they make up a large part of your life and it would take a monumental act of will to eliminate them now.

We need an enormous amount of resolve and energy to surmount our passivity and stop or change these patterns, even if they cause us suffering. For most people, change has a negative valence; they would rather continue in a familiar situation than risk the feelings of panic and emptiness and the possibility of catastrophe that they associate with change.

David, for example, had worked for fifteen years for a successful academic publishing company and had achieved a high level of seniority and job security. He did a good job, but he found the highly specialized books about military history that the company produced to be very boring. Most of David's friends thought of him as a success; if his work was a bit staid, at least it paid the bills. He had thought about leaving for years, but never treated the idea seriously. One day, through the publishing grapevine, he heard of a startup company that was going to produce interactive CD-ROMs about health. Now here was something David thought could have real meaning for himself and for other people. He approached them with the proposal that they hire him as managing editor. The company was very excited about having David's experience and talent behind them. Although they could not match the money he was making, they offered him some stock options and the chance for a creative career. He jumped at it. Changing to a more risky job at forty-five seemed foolish to some of his friends, but David found ample reward in having created a situation where he looked forward to going to work every day.

Does the theme of inertia strike a chord deep within you? Perhaps you find yourself spinning your wheels in a relationship that began with great promise, or stagnating in a job that is light-years away from the brilliant career you once envisioned for yourself. It's not impossible to break the pull, but it does take some serious thought and the determination to take responsibility for how you are going to deal with the events of your life. You don't have control over everything that happens to you, but you do have control over how you handle it.

Changing Your Love Plot

You can change your love plot by examining your fear of being seen and known by another—in short, by examining your fear of love. The more you can recognize your part in diminishing your love plot, the more you can change it—for example, you may be hypercritical, not truly present with your lover, or dishonest about why you are in the habit of seeking out partners whose intimacy problems are larger than your own. As you address your own fears of love, your love plot will naturally blossom. Let's look at how two people, Jeremy and Ruby, changed their love plots.

Jeremy and Jocelyn: From "A Hollow Marriage" to "Passionate Love"

Jeremy, forty-five, was a successful photographer. He and his wife, Lauren, who was five years younger, had been married for seventeen years. Lauren had forgone a career to raise their two sons, who were now teenagers. Jeremy was interested in the history of photography and sought always to branch out in the kind of photography he did—reading, taking classes, going to exhibits.

When their children entered high school, Lauren leaped at the chance to go to work. She got her real estate license and was soon working long hours. She was busy with her clients from early morning until late at night seven days a week—scouting property, showing homes, dealing with bankers and contractors, getting new listings. Although she complained about her hours, her clients, and the market, she loved making deals and making money. She had finally acquired the power and substance she had dreamed of when she was busy raising the boys, and she thrived on it.

Jeremy had been devoted to his children, but felt lonely and empty at home. His world and his wife's world no longer coincided. Sex was infrequent and unsatisfying. He tried to invigorate it by reading sex manuals for married couples, but that didn't work. He bought sexy lingerie for Lauren, but it seemed only a sad symbol of what was missing in their relationship. Lauren seemed to accept the diminishing of their sexual connection as inevitable. He suggested to her that they go to couples counseling. They went a few times, but they didn't get anywhere. Jeremy says:

> I was teaching a night class in basic photography at the university extension. On the first night I was immediately drawn to one of the students, this interesting looking woman who

seemed to be passionate about photography. I couldn't believe my nerve, but after class I started a conversation with her. Her name was Jocelyn, she was forty-eight, and she'd been a widow for just two years. She told me that she had always dreamed of studying photography, but had been too busy working. When her husband died, she suddenly found that she had enough of a financial cushion to pursue her interests.

More quickly than either of them believed possible, they began an affair. Jeremy found that when he was with Jocelyn, he could express his deepest thoughts and feelings. Suddenly he felt blazingly, powerfully alive again. He saw Jocelyn's flaws without idealizing her; he was able to integrate the bad into the good without splitting his vision of her. Feeling seen, cared for, and treasured by her gave him a sense of peace he'd been starved for. He thought of her as a soul mate and wanted to make a new life with her.

He saw that his marriage had become hollow and passionless—he and his wife were truly just good friends. He told Lauren about his feelings for Jocelyn. After the initial shock was over, she responded, "We make a great team. Think about the children and our years together. Don't be rash! This affair will burn out. What we have is far more real and durable than your infatuation for Jocelyn." When Lauren saw that Jeremy was unconvinced, she lost it, and wrecked his studio in a blind rage.

At this point Jeremy was tempted to cut her off, but he didn't. He forgave Lauren, remaining compassionate to her pain, and remembered her many wonderful traits. He moved out of their house but stayed in close, supportive contact with Lauren and the children. They met weekly and he helped her to go into therapy during this transition. Together, they mourned the ending of their marriage.

Eventually Lauren accepted their new relationship of deep friendship. Jeremy, now married to Jocelyn, began doing the photography for the brochures for her new multimillion-dollar property listings. They salvaged what was good in their relationship and remained in each other's lives in new roles.

Ruby and Jurgen: From "I'm Never Appreciated" to "You Know My Most Intimate Self"

Jurgen, a thirty-year-old blind jazz guitarist, met Ruby, a forty-year-old recording engineer, at the studio where he was recording tracks for a friend's CD. Jurgen had just been dumped by his last girlfriend because of his financial insecurity and, in part, because of his disability. Ruby was a big woman who struggled with her weight. Her husband had recently left her for a woman half her age and half her size, and she was feeling pretty bad about herself.

Ruby and Jurgen hit it off immediately, but both were terrified of any passionate involvement. One night they were both working late at the studio, and one thing led to another until they found themselves making out on the floor of the sound studio. After that, they were never apart for more than a few hours.

Ruby found the fact that Jurgen had to "look" at her with his fingers a complete turn-on. All her life she had been ashamed of her body, and here was someone who delighted in it. Jurgen was thrilled that his blindness was so completely accepted by a woman. Their passion was fueled by the fact that they communicated unreservedly in bed. They both realized that they had previously chosen people who wouldn't really open them up and "see" them.

Together, Ruby and Jurgen blossomed. Everyone told Ruby that she had never looked better, and she knew it was true. Instead of being ashamed of her voluptuous dimensions, she felt proud and sensuous. And with Ruby's encouragement, Jurgen began composing, something he had always wanted to do.

Changing Your Mastery Plot

In the world of work and mastery, unlike many other areas of human action, you can usually see a direct relationship between the effort you put in and the result or reward you get back. The following two stories show how it is possible to change your mastery plot.

Evan: From "I'm Secure at Work, but Bored to Tears" to "I'm Doing Something I Love and Getting Paid for It"

Evan, a fifty-year-old tenured biology professor, lived with his lover, Frank, an antiques dealer and appraiser. Evan was the first member of his family to go to college, and he had struggled financially to complete graduate school. His professorship was a dream come true. Yet he was a man of wide and passionate interests who loved nothing better than to investigate the history and provenance of the furniture and art objects that Frank came across in his estate appraisals. Folk art had become his particular interest, especially quilts. While he continued to teach biology, he researched and wrote a charming and informative book on Amish quilts that proved surprisingly popular, although his colleagues felt he should have stayed with a subject closer to biology:

> I guess it was their reaction to the quilt book, which I loved, that made me take a second look at academia. The politics, which I had tried to ignore, were petty, and teaching was getting to be more and more of a grind. I wanted to be out in the "real world."

The original mastery plot Evan had mapped out for himself based on his first love, biology, had a tenured professorship as a satisfying and appropriate long-term goal. But teaching had become a chore; it was no longer authentic for him, and he had little interest in doing biological research. Evan had to decide whether he wanted to stay in a secure, reasonably rewarding life without risks or worries, or to venture out and create something new.

> I agonized for a long time. Academia had been good to me. I really knew my subject, and it seemed a shame to throw it all away. But I knew in my gut that if I didn't take more risks I would consider myself a coward, and my life would always feel constricted.

What Evan needed was the freedom to change his plot. After a lot of thought, he realized that his present field of mastery held the key to his freedom: he wrote a book of biology experiments designed for use in elementary schools. From the book's sales he derived a modest but consistent annual income, almost as much as his professor's salary.

> I couldn't believe it—I was free, and I hadn't had to cut myself off irrevocably from my past to do it. Frank and I were able to spend more time traveling. We went up the Amazon, collected textiles in Morocco, and traveled extensively in Thailand. I fell in love with the Thai people, and I started a small business there exporting textiles to the United States.

Between his fledgling business and his book's sales, Evan realized that he could survive financially without teaching, although his fate would be less secure. After long deliberation he quit his academic position so that he could live for part of each year in Thailand. He gave up security in favor of authenticity, and the trade-off permitted an evolution in his mastery plot.

Samantha: From "I Can't Do Anything Right" to "I Can Do It If I Set My Mind to It"

As a girl, Samantha was highly intelligent but also severely dyslexic. Unfortunately, her disability was not recognized until very late, and her teachers and classmates assumed that she was not very bright. She was miserable.

They put me in the dummy classes. I was bored out of my mind. After twelve years of being treated like an idiot, I was pretty well convinced that I was. It took me hours to decipher the words in my textbooks, and what was the point? My grades were so bad that I didn't have a hope in hell of going to a four-year college. My parents were humiliated that their daughter wasn't living up to their standards. They couldn't conceive of an intelligent person who didn't read and write well.

Samantha's lack of confidence dampened her aspirations and led her to aim no higher than a two-year certificate at a junior college, despite her intelligence and curiosity. Finding a good job without a college degree was nearly impossible, so Samantha went to work selling a luxury cosmetics line at a department store. She was hired because she was personable, attractive, and represented the company's products well. At the training seminars that the company held for its sales staff, Samantha was eager, interested, asked a lot of questions, and got herself noticed by the company's management.

When a job opened up as a receptionist at company headquarters, I jumped at it. I began to realize that my dyslexia might have closed the doors of academic achievement, but I wasn't stupid. I figured I had a better chance of success in a business setting, where what you produced was more important than how well you could read from a book. I got a lot of strokes, and I began to think I might be able to make something of myself after all.

Samantha didn't give up on reading altogether, however. She began listening to books on tape and following along with written text to improve her reading skills. After a year as a receptionist, Samantha had made such a good impression that she was hired as a secretary to the vice-president of research and development. In her new job, much to her surprise, she became interested in the chemistry of the products that the company developed and sold. Her reading was still a little slow, but her intelligence, reliability, judgment, and initiative led her boss to delegate more and more responsibility to her. Her employer came to value her opinion, and asked her to analyze and report on new products, projects, and ideas. Samantha functioned as a gateway, and the projects she selected to put on her boss's desk were consistently promising.

Realizing that the whole department, not just the vice-president, would benefit from her ability to identify new products and good ideas, the company created a job for her.

I had my own office and assistant in the research and development department—unbelievable! I was feeling more and more confident by the day, but sometimes I was frustrated by my inability to understand certain technical points. It suddenly occurred to me—and I mean for the first time in my life—that I wasn't dumb. I could see how hard I had worked to get where I was. I realized that this was just another opportunity for me, and I got the company to pay for me to take some classes in chemistry at night school.

This time she knew exactly what she wanted from school. She no longer mistook her reading disability for low mental ability, and she made sure her teachers didn't, either. Her studies gave her ideas for new products, which she took to the research staff. With their help, she prepared a presentation of a new product line to the president and board. They loved it, and made her a vice-president in charge of the new line.

Samantha was able to transform her mastery plot from dismal failure to innovative success by examining and revising her core beliefs. Instead of taking others' opinion of her at face value, she found a way to change the criteria by which she judged herself, and redescribed what it meant to be intelligent.

Mastery and Relationships: A Warning

Because mastery centers on you and some*thing* rather than you and some*one,* mastery is an impossible plot in the domain of relationships. This is not to say that relationships are not susceptible to improvement, nor that relationship skills and plot revision techniques, such as redescription and "reading" others better, are not learnable. However, your relationships with others, particularly children, have their own plots and are not the appropriate place for practicing mastery.

Why are relationships so resistant to the mastery that skill brings? Because anything that has to do with someone else is not in your control. You can transform yourself, but you are setting yourself up for disappointment if you think that you alone can change a relationship.

Relationships are a chancy source of validation and increased self-esteem, but mastery is always reliable. When you work on your skills outside of relationships, you gain the confidence you need to hold your own with other people and in the world at large. In fact, this is the best argument I know of for women working outside the home. As mastery grows, coherence and identity strengthen as well.

Changing Your Loss Plot

Loss is inevitable. There is no way around it but through it. One of the ways to change your loss plot is to work on accepting the knowledge you already possess: that no one gets everything. No one is spared his or her share of sickness, death, betrayal, and abandonment. No one wants to chase loss; but to truly accept loss is also to savor the richness it brings to your understanding of life and its mysteries. Let's take a look at how two people, David and Corrina, handled their loss plots.

David: From "Everything I Touch I Screw Up" to "I Can Grieve My Losses"

David, a forty-three-year-old plumber, drank steadily for twenty years before he ever tried seriously to quit. What began as social, recreational drinking had quickly become a deep-seated alcohol dependency, although few suspected because he rarely appeared to be drunk.

David was a handsome, bright, personable man, not much given to introspection, who had always been very successful with women. He thought of himself as just a regular guy, one who liked to party a little more than most and had some problems in his marriage, but nothing serious. He saw his drinking and womanizing as part of his virile "man's man" image. He didn't realize that escape had long ago become a full-fledged plot that had outstripped all the others in his life.

> I liked drinking. I like playing around. I didn't try to change until my wife finally got fed up and talked about leaving me—now I wonder what took her so long. I was scared, and I really wanted to stay sober. I went to Alcoholics Anonymous

meetings almost every day, and I managed to stay sober for six months. I was pretty proud of myself, and so was my wife. Then all hell broke loose. One day, out of the blue, my father had a heart attack and died. I went on a bender that made my other benders look like a Club Med vacation. I was drunk for weeks, day and night. I stopped going to work, I stopped eating, I woke up in strange hotel rooms with no idea how I'd gotten there.

When it was finally over and the dust had settled, David's wife had moved out and filed for divorce, taking their seven-year-old daughter. David immediately moved in with a woman he had been seeing off and on during his marriage. She had drinking problems of her own, and had no interest in reforming him. Together, they stayed more or less loaded for a year; David functioned in a kind of dream state fueled by alcohol, grief, and denial. His drinking gradually increased until one night while driving drunk he got into a car accident. Three cars, including his own, were totally destroyed. Miraculously, no one was seriously injured. But David woke up in the hospital knowing he had hit rock bottom.

Man, I was a mess. I always thought that only weak people needed help, like a shrink, but now I had to talk to someone or really go nuts. I started seeing a therapist. I started going to AA meetings again, and this time I got a sponsor. It's hard to get to me, but I finally had to take a cold, hard look at myself. I realized all my life I had been medicating myself into oblivion with alcohol and sex, and I had no idea what I was feeling. I had a long way to go.

David learned in therapy that he had no trustworthy point of view, no reliable narrator who could voice all his intense and often contradictory feelings. He saw that his drinking helped him to abandon himself to each extreme in turn, always denying the reality of the other. Underneath the urge to drink were invariably frightening, powerful emotions. Without the alcohol, there was no mediator between himself and these emotions. He needed to learn to navigate through the turbulent waters of his fears, regrets, and losses without succumbing to the urge to mask them or turn them into something more acceptable.

He was able to find in therapy a container strong enough to hold all his volatile, unacceptable, terrifying feelings as well as his positive ones. This container was his narrator, who derived his strength from truthfulness—from not lying about, hiding, or distracting himself from his vulnerability. He had always worried about what to do with these emotions if they ever "got loose"; he now saw that once he had acknowledged each emotion in his talks with the therapist, he didn't need to "do" anything more with them. He needed to face them, admit their presence, and experience them. For the first time, David had an honest narrator; he worked at this with the help of the therapist's "third-person omniscient" point of view.

He also worked on accepting his father's death, which entailed an enormous amount of grief and loss. He examined his treatment of friends, lovers, and relatives and learned how to express his feelings toward them in a responsible and constructive way. To those whom he had hurt during his years of drinking he finally made amends. All his life, David saw, he had been entirely self-absorbed. To right the balance, he volunteered to help feed the homeless at a shelter twice a week.

David's losses were almost total: his wife and child, his father, his driver's license, his savings, and the loving and comfortable life he had previously known. David found that by allowing himself to grieve over what he had lost and let the painful feelings wash over him, he was able to appreciate what he still had and to build a more satisfying, more positive future.

Corrina: From "Disaster Can Come Out of the Dark and Strike at Any Time" to "In Tragedy There Can Be Learning and Beauty"

We left Corrina earlier in this chapter, when she had encountered a traumatic plot breaker: through no fault of her own, her car had struck and killed a man. Although she was exonerated of any responsibility, she was emotionally devastated. Corrina put her life on hold for months, burying herself in remorse and guilt. She felt she would never be able to get on with her life, and in some sense it was true: her life would never be the same. Finally, with the help of friends, she realized she needed to work through what had happened.

> I decided that running away wouldn't help me. I had to confront this man's death and start the healing process. So I tried to find out all I could about him. I knew that he was a priest, and that his name was Father Frank Connery. I went to the divinity school where he had taught, and was welcomed warmly by the rector. I was overwhelmed with guilt and sorrow, but I was moved when he explained that he had been wanting to contact me and didn't know how. "All of Father Frank's family are praying for you," he told me, and then he gave me a photograph of Father Frank. I was stunned. I had steeled myself for the worst, and I had gotten this.

When Corrina went back to see the head priest a few weeks later, he gave her letters from Father Frank's niece, who was concerned only about Corrina's welfare and expressed no blame. She took care to point out that her uncle had been very ill, was in severe pain and often disoriented. Corrina asked to read the writing that Father Frank had published and continued her correspondence with the niece.

There had been a trauma, one that divided the lives of everyone touched by it into a "before" and "since." But as each of them incorporated the other into his or her life in a genuine way, they were able to transcend the tragedy. In Corrina's experience we see how a plot-breaking event can be transformed by acknowledging and embracing it instead of fleeing.

Exercises for Chapter 8

Finding Your Steps

Select one of the turning points in your love or work life, such as deciding to have a baby, moving to another city, going back to school and changing careers, breaking up with your lover, getting a divorce, and so on. Go back over the process that led you to this conclusion and try to list the steps. It may be difficult to identify specific steps, particularly the "first step." Accepting responsibility for your own part in larger patterns of behavior makes it much easier to trace the causes. (For example, "I always thought I didn't want kids. When my mother died, even though I wasn't very close to her, I felt alone in a way I never had before. Then I started hanging out with a friend from work and her eight-year-old daughter and saw the wonderful connection they had. Somehow I found myself thinking that raising a child was too important an experience to miss out on.")

Movement in Plot

Choose a major movement in your plot—from drunkenness to sobriety, timidity to brazenness, simplicity to pretentiousness, pretentiousness to simplicity, satisfaction to dissatisfaction, and so on.

1. Write down the major steps. For example, "I watched my parents drink, my friend and I stole some liquor from her parents' liquor cabinet, two years later I went to a party and somebody handed me a beer" and so on.
2. Now write a paragraph describing the progression in more emotional terms. For example, "I felt like a captive audience when my parents drank. I hated how they made me listen to them repeat themselves and cry over the past. When I was terrified at parties, drinking a beer made me feel more grown up, less vulnerable," and so on.

Revising Your Core Beliefs

Recall a story you repeatedly told about yourself in your twenties (for example, how your parents never understood you). Write a paragraph to tell it. Name the core belief that story is supporting ("No one understands me").

1. Now take a moment to reflect on how you have revised that account in the intervening years, and write the new version.
2. Has there been a significant change? What core belief does the story now bespeak? Are you satisfied with it?

Plot Breakers

Describe in one paragraph either a trauma or a positive plot breaker that you have experienced, one that has clearly divided your life into "before" and "since."

1. Make two lists: one list of things you used to believe were true about yourself and the world "before" (for example, "Bad things only happen to bad people"), and then another list of things you believe are true about yourself and the world "since" (for example, "It doesn't matter how good you are, disaster can always strike").
2. Compare the two lists. What do they say about how your self and your world were shaken up?

Inertia

Plot is defined by character, and character is defined by action. Even if nothing is "happening," you are "agreeing" to that inaction. Remember, patience is an overrated virtue.

1. List three situations in your life that are unsatisfying or boring, but where you maintain the status quo (jobs and relationships are good places to look).
2. Short of complicating your plot with escape, list small positive actions you could take to change your role in these situations and break the inertia.

9

Twice-Told Tales: Telling and Retelling the Story of Your Life

> When we are really honest with ourselves, we must admit our lives are all that really belong to us. So it is how we use our lives that determines the kind of men we are.
> —Cesar Chavez

We explain ourselves to others through stories—stories of the events of our lives. But the true function of the story is not to convey the content, but rather *what it reveals about who we are*. A well-functioning plot has to reveal the narrator's character, and each story dealing with a major plot must depict the narrator's relationship to the ongoing complications of human life. When we're doing it right, we become modern-day Scheherazades, not only telling our tales of wonder but also living them, as fully dimensional people.

By now, you should be listening to the stories people tell you, and the stories you tell about yourself, in a very different way from when you started this book. When we realize that we are telling the stories of our lives, and that *we have the power to tell the story differently,* we realize that we have the power to change our lives.

For example, Beth's mother was a narcissist. She was interested only in herself, and was very uncaring toward Beth. Because deep down Beth wished her mother had been more loving, she had resisted speaking about her mother's behavior. Her growing understanding of plot making and storytelling, and her skills at reading people, changed the way she was able to think about her mother:

> Even if you've changed your plot in your own mind regarding certain people in your life, you haven't committed yourself to it until you act it out with the people around you. In my case, changing my plot didn't mean merely realizing that my mother had been uncaring toward me all these years, something I never allowed myself to see; it meant that I had to be *telling that story to others.*
>
> From my own experience, I imagine that a lot of people want the unchangeable parts of their stories (for example, that their mother is and always has been uncaring), to be different. For years I knew my mother was uncaring toward me, but I didn't speak about it, except ambivalently. I think a strong reason for this was the unwillingness of people around me to accept something as awful as an uncaring mother! I saw two therapists, and both commented that I never spoke at all about my mother in therapy (of course, they never pushed me further on that, other than to say it was interesting).
>
> Within the structure of plotting, however, I recently began telling the story I have always believed about my mother—that she was incapable of caring for anyone other than herself. For me, accepting the unchangeable parts of my plot has given me a greater feeling of control over things I know I can change. Not accepting the truth of how I was treated slowed me up for years. I was waiting around for things I had no control over—my mother's behavior—to change.

Plot making has taught me very strongly about the roles we play in one another's lives. I have learned that I have more control over my plot if I let people know, in words and actions, what roles they play in my life. This requires me to pay attention to other people's words and actions, and sometimes to make decisions about their characters that I have been reluctant to make—for example, that they are uncaring, selfish, dishonest.

Speaking to people about the roles they play in your life sounded very difficult to me, because I am more accustomed to finding indirect ways out of unpleasant situations. I see now how much I gave up by doing that. From plotting, I have learned that the way to enact my true plot with people is always to focus on the present. Now, if I'm having a conversation with a friend and I'm annoyed about what she's saying, I state what I'm feeling and get off the phone, instead of finding an excuse to get off the phone and feeling furious when I hang up. This way of dealing with people is self-preserving.

With family, I've learned that speaking about the past is futile, other than to illustrate the longevity of a pattern that persists into the present. The past does not have to be lifted and expunged—the thought of that happening probably contributes to the resistance people feel about being truthful to family members. Talking to my mother more assertively about who I am and how she affects me has made me feel more alive in her presence, whereas in the past I had felt very lethargic and depressed around her.

Just as we learn about characters in novels from how they respond to the situations the author has set up for them, real life is filled with situations we can learn from. Often, what we regard as our "problems" can be reframed into lesson plans. When we look at life in this way we begin to understand that to learn from situations is to change how you will narrate your story, and that in turn will change your story.

Successful plotting depends on our willingness to scrutinize our stories, to look for patterns that reveal the deeper stories we are enacting, and to rethink the reasons we behave as we do—reasons we have taken at face value. This means hard work, honesty, and fairness to yourself and others. When you find yourself stuck in a trite plot, such as a love plot that continually ends in rejection, you have to ask yourself how you may be contributing to this situation (for example, Why do I always pick losers?), but remember to be fair to yourself (don't ask, Why am I such a loser?). And never take responsibility for things that don't belong to you, such as someone else's inability to respond with love.

Getting Your Plot Back on Track

The author of fiction is, by definition, always in control of the plot. As narrators of our own life plots, however, we are seldom so lucky. We don't know beforehand how a given situation will work out. We are all too frequently unconscious of our real motives and the motives of others. We can't anticipate the airplane that falls from the sky and smashes our house to smithereens while we're on vacation, and we can't control the comings and goings of other people, no matter how well we know and love them. As a consequence, our plots often take unexpected detours, become repetitive, or may even come to a screeching halt.

Our plots can get off track in three ways:

1. When we don't take responsibility for our own plots—by blaming others for our problems, by assuming the role of a victim, by being passive, or by assuming that we play no part in a problematic situation.
2. When we can't differentiate between our idea of something, such as marriage or children, and the reality of it (for example, what I think children should feel about their

mothers versus what my son Billy actually feels about me).
3. By not observing in ourselves and others the mismatch between actions and words.

If you find yourself stuck in a plot that seems wildly divergent from the one you had in mind for yourself, you may be able to identify the problem by addressing these three points. For example, Terry, a struggling fashion designer, complained to anyone who would listen about her boyfriends' lack of ambition, her succession of intolerant roommates, her stingy parents (they refused to help pay her health club bill), and her sadistic employer (who wouldn't give her the days off she needed to relax in the Bahamas). Not surprisingly, she shortly found herself without friends, a place to live, a job, or sympathy. Her plot completely broke down, and, alone and frightened, she was forced to take an honest look at herself:

> I tried therapy, but even the therapists got sick of hearing me complain about my life. Finally, a friend of mine told me about how we story our lives, and something just clicked. For the first time in my life, I was able to stand outside myself and take a good look. And let me tell you, it was not a pretty sight.
>
> I certainly wasn't taking responsibility for my actions—I was blaming my mistakes on everyone but me. It seems incredible that four roommates could have kicked me out and I still persisted in believing there was something wrong with them.
>
> And I saw that I was mistaking my idea of things for the reality—especially in my work. When I set out to be a fashion designer I thought it would be glamorous and exciting. I knew I was talented, but I didn't realize that a lot of other people were talented too. I expected my boss to give me whatever I wanted because I was this attractive, talented person. What I didn't realize was that the job was hard work, that I'd be competing with other designers, that the bottom line was what I produced, not who I was.

The gap between my words and my actions was huge. I'm embarrassed to this day. My problem wasn't misreading others, it was misreading myself. It was hard, but I began to change the way I was telling my stories. I tried to take responsibility for everything that happened to me (I went a little overboard with that at first—it wasn't my fault that a power failure made me late to an important client meeting), and I was really blown away by the way my direction began to change when I did that.

As Terry retold her story to herself, taking appropriate responsibility for events, closing the gap between her words and her actions, and looking clearly at the reality she was experiencing instead of only feeling worse, she actually began the process of making changes and feeling better. As she gained confidence in her ability to grow, she began to recognize that the future offered her many possibilities she had never thought about before.

Getting Yourself Out of a Trite Plot

You know you're stuck in a trite plot when you can see the rest of your life unfolding before your eyes and the very thought of it makes you want to either burst into tears or run like hell. Usually, these trite plots are not of our own making but are based on someone else's ideas of what our life should be like. These may be the ideas of parents, of society, or of our mate, but one thing is certain: they are not our own.

Getting out of a trite plot is similar to getting your plot back on track—you need to take responsibility, differentiate between the idea of something and its reality, and match words to action—but it may take even more effort and hard work to extricate yourself. The danger in changing a trite plot is the temptation to flee into a trite solution—the stifled housewife who, feeling unappreciated, abandons her family; the man who, feeling angry that his parents are still running his life, cuts them off completely—instead of making a responsible change.

For example, Betsy had been married to the same man for thirty-five years. Her husband was a successful advertising executive, and they lived in a large home in an exclusive community, where she was a member of the Junior League and on the board of several charities. When her husband died and left her with a lot of money, everyone—including her two grown children—expected her to continue living in the big house, her life unchanged. But although she had never voiced it, Betsy had always dreamed of working with the disadvantaged rather than just giving them money, something her husband would never have understood. Now, feeling liberated from her old life, she moved to a cozier home and bought another building, where she opened a residence for homeless mothers and children. Betsy managed the shelter, cooked the food, and worked to help the women get jobs and find permanent homes.

What to Do When Your Plot Gets Stuck

When we feel stuck in our plots—spinning our wheels in frustration—it's usually because we are stuck in our viewpoint. The best thing to do here is to redescribe the situation, reframing it in terms that allow you to see that same set of circumstances in a completely new way (for example, being free to see that, upset as you were at the time, not getting that job or being rejected by that lover was a good thing because of what happened to you instead).

Marlene, fifty-five, developed serious health problems and had to quit her job as a bookkeeper. She couldn't manage on the small fixed income she received from disability, and was forced to live in a small cottage behind her aunt's house. For the first month after she moved, she felt very depressed that this was how her life had turned out. Then, one morning, she awoke with the realization that she could redescribe her situation. For many years she had been writing a novel in what she had bitterly called her "spare time." Now, however, she realized that with a little imaginative redescription, she could conceptualize herself as having moved to a writer's colony. After all, she was finally free to write all day, with no distractions, and her basic needs were being met. With this new plot, her depression lifted and she was more productive as a writer than she had ever been.

What to Do When You've Read Someone Wrong

If you are really paying attention to words and actions, you may find that when more of a person's character is revealed, it may no longer fit with or may even obliterate what you think is true about that person. (Sometimes it even feels like your friend has been replaced by his evil twin!) It's no fun to be surprised in this way. If your new knowledge of someone throws your old plot out the window, try this: retell your old stories about the person using your new knowledge. This is especially important when you've been betrayed.

For example, Alexandra suspected that her husband occasionally had affairs, but she never spoke to him about it and just hoped that she was wrong. In her heart, she felt that she must be letting him down in some way. One day, seemingly out of nowhere, he told her that he wanted to end their marriage. From a mutual friend, who now felt free to speak, she discovered that he had numerous affairs not only during their marriage but all the time they were engaged. With this new information, she began to revise her view of her marriage and its problems. She realized, in retrospect, that her real mistake was staying in the marriage as long as she had, and in not asking him point blank about his philandering. She regretted her role in maintaining the status quo.

These are the important points to keep in mind about reading people:

1. Character is revealed in deed and action, not in talk and self-description.
2. Character must be revealed over time, through increments.
3. If you are invested in a false story about a person, loss is inevitable.
4. People's actions never spring out of nowhere; when they are unexpected, they come from a subplot of which you were unaware.
5. Don't forget to test your hypotheses about people by asking questions and expecting answers. Always ask more than one yes or no question, and don't forget to follow up a yes or no answer with the question, "Why?"

Taking Risks

The ability to take chances determines how creative your plot can be. Tolerance of risk is essential to the makeup of the narrator. As Bob Dylan says, "He not busy being born is busy dying."

Risks can be obvious or hidden. Hidden risks have to do with the price of missed opportunities. Although trying for something and failing to achieve it is very painful, it is also an act of courage and often allows you to redefine failure as something that happens to everyone on the road to success.

Creatively plotting your life means taking responsibility for your actions, living life actively rather than passively, and this inevitably involves taking risks. Security and dependence must not always be the narrator's prime motivation. The ability to tolerate risk is necessary to autonomy and freedom.

Of course, only a fool would advocate wanton risk. You don't have to behave psychically like Evel Knievel! Too much risk stifles creativity as surely as too little. Instead, you need to choose risks carefully, opening your eyes to the dangers without giving in to terror at the possibilities. When you consciously choose to take a risk, you can no longer play the role of victim. You have to say to yourself, "I'm choosing this and it may not work out." Nothing worthwhile comes without risk.

Cut to the Chase

People often think about the story of their life when it breaks down. Some painful or overwhelming event, which may have come as a complete surprise, has shaken up your view of your story. Your narrative, already brittle because it was constructed from images and ideas rather than from examined experience, crumbles. What you cannot imagine as true about you is often where your greatest vulnerability lies. These are your blind spots, and they weaken your ability to assess and change your plot.

The ongoing process of plotting provides a cohesive narrative framework that blends past and present. The basic building block of this narrative is the application of language to events, describing experiences in a way that both reassures and creates mastery.

Like a detective, you will be able to link seemingly unrelated events from the present to the past. Although people often lose track of when and why their emotional reactions got stirred up, there is a logic to emotions. They don't just descend on you for no reason. Plotting helps you discover what, for you, was emotionally meaningful about an experience by seeing patterns and determining which events are plottable, in what order, and with what relative importance.

The narrative must be supple in order to accommodate the possibility of change. If it's rigid, the plot will just collapse. A supple narrative framework allows the unforeseen to pop up, and provides ways to survive and affirm it. You should enjoy being surprised by life!

Certain stories seem prerecorded, quotable phrases produced over and over for public consumption without the slightest change, so that the narrator is no longer connected to what he or she is saying. These stories are a performance, not an interaction. The speaker is not relating to the listener. In the "authorized version" of a person's childhood, marriage, or important relationships, for instance, one can often hear a rehearsed kind of language, as though something were being protected or defended. We show one self to the world, while at times our real self lies behind defenses—namely, the stories we tell. Defenses always hide the plot of the self.

One of the healing aspects of plotting is seeing your life make sense as a narrative. Finding out where certain feelings and beliefs came from permits redescription—not just in the present but continuing into the future as the narrator evolves. A supple narrative is fluid, shapely, capable of movement. It permits an ongoing understanding of the past. It allows you to return again and again to important events in your life with evolving understanding. Writer Jill Johnston describes this process in an article in *The New York Times Book Review* entitled "Fictions of the Self in the Making":

> Recently a friend wrote to me about his dead father, saying that at thirty he thought he was really beginning to understand him. Now he says, at sixty-five, he's finding ever-new aspects: that is, the facts he remembers are the same, but his present-day interpretations are different. His interpretation of the same event is different today from what it was in 1985, 1975, 1969, 1955, etc. . . . With the facts, we can endlessly

move them around, make them do things, act on them, pitch them in different contexts. As we remake the past, we alter the way we see ourselves in the present and the way we cast ourselves into the future.

Plot-altering change occurs in steps. First, we learn to identify and relinquish aspects of old patterns or stories. We make an effort to locate emotional patterns and grasp the ways in which we continuously recreate the same plot. Second, because the content of change is taking responsibility, we come to appreciate our contribution to our own difficulties, and become willing to accept the knowledge that we have played some part in originating our present distress. Third, we start to act out some small aspect of our patterns differently, and observe what that increment of change brings. We must practice, maintain, and generalize this pattern. Practice requires deciding again and again to change, committing ourselves to it over and over. The burdens of responsibility and self-consciousness never disappear.

Finally, we must enact the revisions we have made to our plots. Sometimes this is extremely difficult with loved ones who have their own competing narratives of who you are and what you should do. Changing our narrative means changing our behavior to back up that new narrative. Although the change may look small on the surface, its narrative possibilities could be enormous.

No one gives up even an inadequate behavior for an unrealized promise until that promise has sufficient scope to lure us to take a risk. Further, as long as we keep putting off trying to change, we don't have to deal with the guilt and sadness that follow our recognition of the part we've played in our own misery.

Change happens when we relinquish an old pattern that we see, in part, as our responsibility. In its place we initiate a new way of thinking, acting, or feeling. As new patterns become more clearly defined and can be compared to the old, we can observe the increments of change and claim greater responsibility. To change is to commit to an action and carry it out; without action, the decision to change hasn't been made. Since change requires you to travel into the unknown, it is often scary. Ultimately, we embark on this journey not because our goals are so worthy or attractive but because to stay where we are has become so painful.

As you look back upon your life, you may find that your narrative of, say, your childhood or your marriage is quite different from your mother's, your sister's, or your mate's. For example, your mom may tell you that you loved that odious tap dancing class—and other family members may present other competing and compelling narratives—but as the author of your own plot you have the power to decide on the best, most inclusive, most believable narrative *for you*. You get to be the final editor of your own story.

Exercises for Chapter 9

Revision

Looking back over past events affords you an opportunity to revise your interpretation, clearing up misconceptions and sometimes releasing guilt and pain in the process. It may be that the way we reacted to an event at the time was the only reaction possible, and then the situation becomes a fixed story in our repertoire. (For example, as a child you thought you were "too demanding" because you wanted your self-absorbed parents to show you some real concern and attention.) Although the interpretation is not totally accurate, you cannot discover this unless you revisit the experience with an open mind. As you grow in maturity and experience, your interpretation of past events may need to be revised to reveal the true feelings and understanding that were hidden beneath the surface. You may already have revised your view of a hurtful situation, but at a time when your perspective, information, and experience were still very limited. Revisiting those experiences again allows us to revise them again, with all our accumulated self-knowledge.

1. Write a paragraph describing one of these "fixed stories" in your repertoire.
2. Now revise the paragraph with an open mind, based on your accumulated self-knowledge. (For example, were you "too demanding," or were you demanding what was rightfully yours but impossible for your parents to give?)

Moving Your Plot Along

Make a list of your assumptions about what will happen to you in the next five years.

1. If any are negative, see if you can revise them from a more positive perspective.
2. Pick one of the positive assumptions and make another list in a way that shows the increments of movement from where you are now to where you want to be—not simply, "I will publish a book" but "I will get up an hour early each day to work on my book," "I will meet with a developmental editor once a month," and so on.

Getting Your Plot Unstuck

Write a paragraph describing your life as it is right now, today, as regards a plot turn you can't seem to get out of. Tell it in the third person, with yourself as a character. (For example, "Greg had been working at the same job for five years. Every night he went back to his wife and six children. Every night dinner was waiting. He thought if he had to do this for one more day he would probably shoot himself." Now go on and write Chapter 2. What might happen?

Crossroads

Projects and relationships that were not feasible for whatever reasons earlier in your life may become more possible later in life. You may discover future options from looking back at "roads not taken" in the past.

1. List as many crossroads from your own life as you can. Write down the path you took and the path not taken (for example, you chose to go to Europe rather than to graduate school; you chose to get married instead of working on your writing).
2. Can you see any possibility of recycling a "road not taken" into the narrative of your life now? Pick one and write a paragraph describing how you could act on it today.

Surprises

Bad memories take up a lot more pages in your plot than good ones. Positive memories tend to fade, unless we remind ourselves of them.

1. Make a list of five experiences in your life that went well, to your surprise.
2. What part did you play in each?
3. Describe your character in light of these events, revising your usual self-description to account for your "surprising" behavior.

Thinking About Risk

Recall the time you didn't do something because you were afraid to risk failure or rejection.

1. Write a paragraph describing what happened.
2. Now rewrite the story as if you had taken the risk. What happened?
3. Was your fear of risk giving you good information? Or was your fear of risk obscuring your real choices?
4. Think about a situation you are currently facing that involves a certain amount of risk. Make two lists: one of possible outcomes resulting from taking the risk, and one of possible outcomes resulting from not taking the risk. Is your fear of this particular risk giving you good counsel or holding you back? How do you feel about the situation now?

You Are a Character in a Novel

After a particularly upsetting experience like failing a big exam or breaking up with someone important or being fired from work, imagine you were reading about a character in a novel rather than yourself.

1. What would feel satisfying to you as a reader and make you sympathetic to the character's plight?
2. How would you want the character to react or not react? What action would you want the character to take?

Keeping a Journal

Keeping a journal is a good way to continue reading and revising your plot. The notebook you have created while reading this book is a good place to start. Many of the exercises can be repeated over time, yielding a new perspective on your life as it continues to evolve. It is particularly useful to reread from time to time what you wrote in your journal about important relationships. You know how things actually turned out with that person, and you can observe with the benefit of hindsight how appropriately you reacted. Rereading allows you to look at yourself with an objective eye. Do you tend to be melodramatic, fair, self-pitying, blaming? Continue to use the new information you learn from reading about yourself to shape your plot as it unfolds. Rethinking the past is a pointless enterprise unless it triggers and informs our growth and change in the present.

Bibliography

Austen, Jane. *Pride and Prejudice.*

Berne, Eric. *Beyond Games and Scripts.* New York: Ballantine, 1976.

Braverman, Kate. "Afterthoughts." In *Hurricane Warnings.* Los Angeles: Illuminati, 1987.

Broyard, Anatole. *Intoxicated by My Illness.* New York: Fawcett, 1992.

Bruner, Edward M. "Experience and Its Expressions." In *The Anthropology of Experience,* edited by Victor W. Turner and Edward M. Bruner. Urbana and Chicago: University of Illinois, 1986.

Cohen, Leonard. *Stranger Music.* New York: Pantheon, 1993.

Coontz, Stephanie. *The Way We Never Were.* New York: Basic Books, 1992.

Coward, Rosalind. *Female Desires.* New York: Grove, 1985.

Crites, Stephen. "Storytime." In *Narrative Psychology,* edited by Theodore Sarbin. New York: Praeger, 1986.

Davis, Murray. *Smut.* Chicago: University of Chicago, 1983.

De Salvo, Louise. *Conceived with Malice.* New York: Dutton, 1994.

Dibell, Ansen. *Plot.* Cincinnati: Writer's Digest Books, 1988.

Egri, Lajos. *The Art of Dramatic Writing.* New York: Simon and Schuster, 1946.

Ellis, John. *Visible Fictions.* London: Routledge and Kegan Paul, 1982.

Fairbairn, W. Ronald D. *Object Relations Theory of Personality.* London: Routledge and Kegan Paul, 1952.

Forster, E. M. *Aspects of the Novel.* New York: Harcourt, Brace and World, 1927.

Gabler, Neil. "Now Playing: Real Life, the Movie." *New York Times,* October 20, 1991.

Gallagher, Winifred. "Midlife Myths." *The Atlantic,* May 1993.

Greenblatt, Stephen. "Storytelling." In *Hiding in Plain Sight,* edited by Wendy Lesser. San Francisco: Mercury House, 1993.

Heilbrun, Carolyn. *Writing a Woman's Life.* New York: Norton, 1988.

Hochschild, Arlie. *The Second Shift.* New York: Viking, 1989.

Houston, Pam. *Cowboys Are My Weakness.* New York: Washington Square Press, 1992.

Jack, Dana Crowley. *Silencing the Self.* Cambridge, Mass.: Harvard University Press, 1991.

Johnston, Jill. "Fictions of the Self." *New York Times Book Review,* April 25, 1993.

Jones, Gerard. *Honey, I'm Home.* New York: Grove Weidenfeld, 1992.

Keen, Ernest. "Paranoia and Cataclysmic Narratives." In *Narrative Psychology,* edited by Theodore Sarbin. New York: Praeger, 1986.

Klein, Melanie. *Envy and Gratitude.* New York: Delacorte, 1975.

———. "Mourning and Its Relation to Manic Depressive States." In *Love, Guilt and Reparation.* New York: Dell, 1975.

Lamott, Anne. *Bird by Bird.* New York: Pantheon, 1994.

Larkin, Philip. *Collected Poems.* New York: Farrar, Straus and Giroux, 1988.

Lawson, Annette. *Adultery.* New York: Basic Books, 1988.

Modleski, Tania. *Loving With a Vengeance.* New York: Methuen, 1982.

Moore, Lorrie. "How to Be an Other Woman." In *Self-Help.* New York: Knopf, 1985.

Person, Ethel. *Dreams of Love and Fateful Encounters.* New York: Norton, 1988.

Price, Reynolds. *A Whole New Life.* New York: Atheneum, 1994.

Radway, Janice. *Reading the Romance.* Chapel Hill: University of North Carolina Press, 1984.

Rorty, Richard. *Contingency, Irony and Solidarity.* Cambridge, Eng.: Cambridge University Press, 1989.

Rose, Phyllis. *Parallel Lives.* New York: Vintage, 1984.

Rushdie, Salman. "One Thousand Days in a Balloon." *New York Times*, December 12, 1991.

Sarbin, Theodore. "A Root Metaphor." In *Narrative Psychology*, edited by Theodore Sarbin. New York: Praeger, 1986.

Schafer, Roy. "Narrative in the Psychoanalytic Dialogue." In *On Narrative*, edited by W. J. T. Mitchell. Chicago: University of Chicago, 1981.

Sheehy, Gail. *New Passages*. New York: Random House, 1995.

Sidel, Ruth. *On Her Own*. New York: Viking, 1990.

Skolnick, Arlene. *Embattled Paradise*. New York: Basic Books, 1991.

Spence, Donald. *Narrative Truth and Historical Truth*. New York: Norton, 1982.

Steele, Robert S. "Deconstructing Realities." In *Narrative Psychology*, edited by Theodore Sarbin. New York: Praeger, 1986.

Taylor, Charles. *The Ethics of Authenticity*. Cambridge, Mass.: Harvard University Press, 1992.

Tisdale, Sallie. "Talk Dirty to Me." *Harper's*, February 1992, 37–46.

Von Franz, Marie. *Puer Aeternus*. Santa Monica, Calif.: Sigo Press, 1970.

Wachtel, Eleanor. "An Interview with Alice Munro." In *The Brick Reader*, edited by Linda Spaulding and Michael Ondaatje. Toronto: Coach House Press, 1991.

Weldon, Fay. *Remember Me*. New York: Ballantine, 1976.

Winnicott, D. W. *Playing and Reality*. Harmondsworth, Eng.: Penguin, 1971.

Index

Sea of Love (film), 99
seduction, in stories, 131–33
self
  authentic/core, 30, 52, 70,
    121–23
  and changing love plots, 192
  childhood, 112
  confirmation of views about,
    37–38
  and core beliefs, 35–39
  and creativity, 96
  and defensive strategies,
    121–23
  evolution of, 35–39
  mature, 61–63
  and plot breakers/trauma, 186,
    187
  popular culture as criticism of,
    158
  and power, 149
  and seduction in storytelling,
    131–33
  sense of, 61–63
  sexual fantasy as revelation
    about, 99–100
  time needed for development
    of, 61–63
  See also narrators
self-esteem
  and change, 197
  and control, 59–60
  and core beliefs, 39, 57
  definition of, 57
  development of, 57
  fluctuation in, 57
  and hope, 57
  and loss plots, 60
  and love plots, 57, 60, 69
  and marriage, 111
  and mastery plots, 57, 60, 197

as motivation for plots, 56, 57,
    59–60
  and pretense, 57
  and risk, 60
  and separation, 59–60
self-image, 38–39, 52, 195–97,
    215–16
self-knowledge, 34–35, 38,
    67–68, 121
self-observation, 42–43
sentimentality, 45–46
separation, 56, 58–60, 61
sex
  as complication of plots,
    97–104, 117
  control of, 98–99
  editing of plots about, 97–98
  exercises about, 117
  fantasies about, 68, 99–100
  in films, 99
  and hackneyed plots, 30
  idealization of, 158
  and love plots, 100–104, 192
  lying about, 98
  and marriage, 71
  in mastery plots, 102–3
  and popular culture plots, 157,
    158
  and power, 71, 99
  as source of self-knowledge,
    67–68
  and violence, 99
Sheehy, Gail, 18
Simpson, O. J., 165
sitcoms, 158–59
Skolnick, Arlene, 107, 108
splitting
  of narration, 174
  and reading others, 137–39,
    153